THE
PIPE
SMOKER

THE PIPE SMOKER

*Being An
Entertaining & Scientific
Treatise on Pipes
&
Tobaccos
With Wholly New
Revelations About
The Pipe Smoker*

John Paul Beaumier
&
Lewis Camp

Illustrations: Jonquille Albin

1817

Harper & Row, Publishers, San Francisco
Cambridge, Hagerstown, Philadelphia, New York
London, Mexico City, São Paulo, Sydney

FIRST EDITION

Designed by Frederick Mitchell

Library of Congress Cataloging in Publication Data

Beaumier, John Paul.
 The pipe smoker.

 Bibliography: p. 139
  1. Tobacco-pipes. 2. Smoking.
I. Camp, Lewis, joint author. II. Title.
GT3020.B4   1980   394.1'4   79-1770
ISBN 0−06−250367−1

80 81 82 83 84 10 9 8 7 6 5 4 3 2 1

CONTENTS

Introduction

PART I: THE PERSONALITY OF THE PIPE SMOKER

1. The Masculine Minority   13
2. Smoking Him Out: Science Looks at the Pipe Smoker   19
3. Behind the Smokescreen:
   The Social Image of the Pipe Smoker   23
4. The Personality of the Pipe Smoker:
   Extravert or Introvert?   29
5. Behind the Image: A Healthy Introvert   35

PART II: WHAT THE BODY SAYS

6. Arousal   45
7. The Pipe of Peace: Relaxation   49
8. Where There's Smoke There's Fire:
   Sex and the Pipe Smoker   55
9. The Meditative Mind Is a Healthy Mind   61

PART III: A SENSUAL GUIDE TO
          THE ART OF PIPE SMOKING

10. The Odor and Taste of Tobacco   69
11. The Look and Feel of the Pipe   77
12. The Caking, Filling, and Lighting of the Pipe   83
13. The Exquisite Pleasure of Puffing   91
14. The Care and Feeding of a Pipe   99

PART IV: THE GRAND WORLD OF PIPES

15. From Soapstone to Calabash Gourds:
    What Pipes Are Made Of   109
16. The Geometry of Pipes: How Pipes Are Made   117

PART V: THE RELIGIOUS AND SYMBOLIC
          ASPECTS OF PIPE SMOKING

17. The Sensuous Symbolism of PipeSmoking   125
18. Sacred and Profane Pipe Smoking   131

References   139

INTRODUCTION

*T*he spread of tobacco and pipe smoking from America to Europe —
and thence to the rest of the world — was an extraordinary
event in human culture. By the end of the sixteenth century in
Europe, the smoking of tobacco in a pipe had become such a popular
pastime that it quickly took its place beside wine, ale, and spirits as
one of the most culturally significant substances in human history.
The pipe provided a new way of ingesting an intoxicating substance:
rather than sipping an alcoholic beverage, one puffed, tasted, and inhaled a pleasant and consciousness-changing smoke.

From its earliest European acceptance, pipe smoking was a subject of intense interest and study. From that time onward there appeared floods of books concerning the marvelous smoking instru-

ment and the magic herb, which American Indians believed to be of divine origin.

Because of its reputed magical and curative properties, Europeans found far more uses for tobacco than merely smoking it in a pipe. They devised ways of chewing it, drinking it, sniffing it, and smoking it in long wrappers, which they called cigars. But the immensely popular—indeed adored—receptacle for the tobacco leaf was the pipe, a wondrous invention that is as ancient as clay and as rich in symbolism as the staff and the miter.

Throughout its long history, pipe smoking has been characterized by one feature of great significance: it has always been a male preoccupation. Of course there are some notorious examples of female pipe smokers; but their very notoriety only serves to prove the rule.

The invention of the cigarette rolling machine in the early twentieth century, combined with the fast-paced lifestyle of the emerging urban-industrial society, served to decimate the once teeming ranks of pipe smokers. There was simply no time to enjoy a pipe, and the quick stimulus of a cigarette took its place with the cup of coffee as the accepted way to gird one's loins to face the rigors of modern life.

The number of pipe smokers diminished very rapidly. As we near the end of the twentieth century, we find that most users of tobacco are cigarette smokers. And, as cigarette consumption has grown in popularity, it has become as much a female as a male prerogative.

But, during this period of widespread and unisex cigarette smoking, a happily stubborn contingent of males—perhaps ten million in North America—continues to extol the pleasures of the pipe. These diehards believe that cigarette smoking is so different from pipe smoking that it does not even merit comparison. In fact, this coterie of pipe smokers claims that the singular pleasures they experience daily are utterly unknown not only to cigarette smokers, but to all nonusers of tobacco.

INTRODUCTION

Pipe smokers constitute a group of a most special kind. They have not succumbed to the almost universal practice of cigarette smoking, and they have remained, without trying, a solidly male group. There is something undeniably male about pipe smoking, just as there is something peculiarly masculine about the attractions of a pipe.

Pipe smokers stand apart from the rest of humanity. They have always been a special group of human beings whose interests and personalities are a bit different from those of their fellows. Of course all of us know this, women in particular. When we think of a pipe smoker we usually have the image of a certain kind of person, someone a little different from other males.

For almost five hundred years, treatises have been written about pipes and tobacco, but nothing has been written about the essential element in the triumvirate: the pipe smoker. So *The Pipe Smoker* is about pipes and it is about tobacco, but it is particularly about the pipe smoker and what it is that makes him different from other humans. Once we come to know some of the compelling reasons for this difference, we will better understand why the infinite varieties of tobaccos and pipes have such special meaning to this special person.

PART I

THE
PERSONALITY
OF THE
PIPE SMOKER

1

THE MASCULINE MINORITY

Another reason for my pipe smoking was that I wanted to be a doctor, and having this idea in mind, I always thought that doctors looked so distinguished smoking pipes.

One other reason was to satisfy my beautiful woman, and she has thusly inspired me to continue my collection.

And a last comment: when traveling, the topics of conversation from one pipe smoking stranger to another are the kinds of tobacco, the different pipes, and how long he has been smoking. Ofttimes this exchange of ideas leads to long and lasting friendships.

—A Georgia pipe smoker

*B*ehold the pipe smoker. He is not like other men. Although the brotherhood of pipe smokers numbers in the millions, it is recognized as a unique group—not only by pipe smokers themselves, but by society at large.

The image is well deserved, for it is no simple matter to smoke a pipe. It requires the smoker to acquire a certain amount of equipment, and to give it a certain amount of time. To begin with, one pipe is not enough. The smoker must have at least two, so that the hot one can be cooled and rested. He must have a humidor or a tobacco pouch, so that the tobacco can be kept at just the right moisture content: if it's too dry, it will burn hot; if it's too wet, it will die. The pipe smoker must also carry matches or a pipe lighter, tools to tamp down the tobacco and clean out the bowl, and a number of pipe cleaners.

No matter how busy he is, the pipe smoker has time to spare and makes full use of it. He practices his art in a leisurely manner—no one ever thinks of a pipe smoker as nervous and fidgety. On the contrary, he is most deliberate and patient. The slow-paced, methodical way in which he goes about preparing and smoking his pipe is essential to a secret pleasure that only other pipe smokers share.

Notice the patient, unhurried way in which he takes out his briar, carefully sniffs its bowl, peers into it looking for leftover tobacco, then briefly cleans out the bowl with his pipe tool and lightly taps the pipe against some pleasantly solid yet yielding surface. A cigarette smoker might easily be a third of the way through his cigarette before the pipe smoker even gets around to opening up his tobacco pouch. And once the pouch is open, there is *still* no rush. The deliberate smoker will reach into his pouch, take a pinch of tobacco, and then—holding the pipe just inside the pouch—poke the first pinch carefully down into the bottom of the bowl. Then, with the same easy pace, he will reach for a second pinch and lay in a second story of tobacco, tamping carefully so that the draught will be easy and unclogged. He will continue adding tobacco until he puts in the final pinch, evening out the last one with the flat of his thumb and the edge of his thumbnail. The pipe is ready. Anyone who would go to such lengths in today's hurried world is indisputably a special sort of person.

It is time to light up, but still there is no haste. The pipe smoker takes out his wooden match or his pipe lighter, strikes the light, and begins a series of careful maneuvers whereby he coordinates flame, pipe bowl, and puffing to ensure that the pipe is lit evenly. First he draws the fire to the center and puffs the tobacco into flame. Then he moves the match around in an easy circle, lighting one spot after another around the periphery of the bowl. These beginning puffs are fairly strong; they are designed to obtain an even-burning bowl with the fire in the center. Once this is achieved, the pipe smoker usually puffs away for a minute or so and then, almost inevitably, the pipe goes out.

This is not a cause of alarm for the imperturbable pipe smoker. He now takes his thumb or pipe tool and lightly tamps down the ashes on top. The first burn-off is completed. Now he can get down to the real business of pipe smoking. He lights up again, carefully, and this times seems to puff a little more lightly. He is now getting into the real business of pipe smoking: pleasure. He settles back, concentrating his attention on the hot, smoking, aromatic bowl. The puffs are light, easy, and practiced. Like the surfer riding his wave, the pipe smoker artfully puffs to create just the right degree of burning—not too fast nor too slow, not too hot nor too light. Now, for fifteen to twenty minutes, the pipe smoker enters into a realm apart, a world of calmness and peace and sensual pleasure.

If an observer from another planet were to come upon the pipe smoker, he would no doubt conclude that this human was performing some kind of a ritual—and of course he would be right. Pipe smoking is not only a pleasure and not merely an art; it is also a complex, time-consuming ritual that is practiced primarily by male Homo sapiens. Many rituals are designed to place human beings in contact with special powers. The pipe smoker, who after careful preparation is embarked on a serene voyage of gently paced puffing, is certainly in communion with a higher spirit.

The ritual nature of pipe smoking gives the pipe smoker a special connection with his fellows. When he sees another man lighting up, his eyes and nose are naturally drawn to the familiar activities. Ignoring any separations of class, profession, or dress, the pipe smoker recognizes in his fellow a bond deeper than these otherwise important social distinctions. Not only does he know that this fellow pipe smoker regularly enjoys the same tranquil pleasure as he himself does, he also knows that they share common traits.

Imagine a crowded room filled with a variety of people: if there are two pipe smokers in that room, you can be sure they will discover each other. One man, perhaps, makes a comment about the other's pipe. In due time, the pipe is handed to him so that he may examine it — looking, touching, sniffing, and peeking into the bowl to check the cake. Because the pipe smoker, like a seeker of the Holy Grail, is eternally and ceaselessly in pursuit of the perfect blend, each will inevitably ask the other what he smokes. Is it an American or an English blend, or a bag of sweet-cured, aromatic cavendish? Perhaps it is a tobacconist's blend of 100 percent white burley, or burley blended with sweet flue-cured Virginia tobacco and a touch of perique.

After the blends have been thoroughly discussed, the pipe smokers will proceed to the cut of the leaf. Pipe tobaccos are cut in different shapes and sizes, according to the varied pleasures of pipe smokers. Each variation, no matter how minor it may seem to the uninitiated, is of major concern to this seeker of fumatory pleasure. The tastes and explorations of the fellowship of pipe smokers are complex and labyrinthine.

This mutual identification and lively interest in exchanging information leads pipe smokers quite easily into the formation of clubs, such as The Universal Coterie of Pipe Smokers, or commercial enterprises like Wally Frank's pipe catalogue. All over Europe and North America club members share the latest news about pipe shapes, materials for pipe making, blends, casing sauces and cuts of tobacco, and newly discovered literature or lore about pipe smoking and pipe smokers.

The serious and well-considered information exchanged by members of these clubs shows that pipe smokers have a very special attitude: they trust one another. The shared experience of smoking a pipe leads to a camaraderie, and wherever and whenever pipe smokers gather together a community immediately forms.

The smoking of a pipe is traditionally an occasion for convivial and fraternal closeness, as it was in the coffee houses of eighteenth-

Figure 1. Nargeeleh. The custom of drawing smoke through water to cool and cleanse it was never practiced by the native Americans or Europeans, though this form of pipe is common throughout Africa and Asia. Its name means coconut and the shell was used by Arab traders to substitute for the dakka pipe smoked by Africans. In India and Persia it was as avidly smoked by women as by men.

century England and the cafés of nineteenth-century Arabic lands. Indeed, this sociability and trust have characterized the community of pipe smokers since the very beginning.

Tobacco smoking originated with the Indians of North America, to whom it was a divine gift to mankind and the long pipe the sacred instrument for sharing that gift. The Indians' pipe was made of red soapstone and a long reed to draw out the smoke. Early French explorers gave the pipe the name calumet, which means "reed."

The French were impressed with the pipe's ritual and social power. Whenever a treaty or mutual compact was to be made, the calumet ritual was essential for sealing the agreement. For each Indian chief to smoke the calumet with other chiefs was sufficient to seal a pact. And for one chief to exchange calumets with another was to establish a pact of nonaggression and fraternity. Inversely, refusal to accept and smoke another's calumet was virtually an act of open hostility and declaration of war.

The calumet was, in every sense, "the pipe of peace." Its power as a token of peace was so great that its possession automatically guaranteed safe passage through territories of hostile tribes. British and French explorers repeatedly found that their lives would be spared if they carried a "peace pipe."

The tobacco pipe had a ritual significance even more profound than the communal and social harmony it promoted. Typically, the calumet was filled in six stages, one for each of the four compass points, one for the heavens above, and one for the earth below. So filled, the pipe represented the universe.

> In filling the pipe, all space (represented by the offerings to the powers of the six directions) and all things (represented by the grains of tobacco) are contracted within a single point (the bowl or heart of the pipe), so that the pipe contains, or really *is* the universe. But since the pipe is the universe, it is also man, and the one who fills a pipe should identify himself with it, thus not only establishing the center of the universe but also his own center; he so "expands" that the six directions of space are actually brought within himself. It is by this expansion that a man ceases to be a part, a fragment, and becomes whole or holy; he shatters the illusion of separateness.[1]

2

SMOKING HIM OUT: SCIENCE LOOKS AT THE PIPE SMOKER

I find smoking a pipe very relaxing and satisfying. It helps me to keep my cool, because before saying or doing anything hasty I stop and light up. This gives you time to think, makes you more composed, and leads to better relations with associates. If this doesn't work, then you bite your pipe stem and not your tongue.

—An Arkansas pipe smoker

*F*or over four thousand years, the pipe smoker has been special. He does not often blush or show anxiety; rather, he seems cool, deliberate, patient, and contemplative. He is perceived as thoughtful and kindly, a man who can be trusted. Is there any basis to this generally accepted image? "Deliberate," "contemplative," "easygoing," "solid," "manly"—does all this sound like the description of a personality type? It most certainly is: it is the personality of the pipe smoker.

If you are a pipe smoker or cigarette smoker, ask yourself the following questions: Do I prefer taking action to planning for action? Would I rate myself as a lively individual? Do I usually take the initiative in making new friends? Would I be unhappy if I were prevented from making numerous social contacts? Am I happiest participating in a scheme that calls for rapid action? Am I inclined to be quick and sure in my actions?

And then try these as well: Do I become so absorbed in whatever I'm doing that I don't like to be interrupted and have to change to something new? Do I feel I can really enjoy myself with friends after I've done my duty and finished whatever task I've had in mind? Do I remain outwardly calm when people around me are disturbed and excited? Do I think that a person who does not live up to the standards he sets himself does not deserve sympathy? Do I always prefer the familiar and certain to taking chances with the new and untried?

According to Burton Shean, who devised these two sets of questions,[2] cigarette smokers are more likely to say yes to the first set of questions; pipe smokers are more likely to say yes to the second set. Shean's survey was designed to bring scientific measurement to the question, "What is the social image of the pipe smoker?" From the answers he received, he concluded that "the traditional image of the pipeman (contemplative, solid, kind, careful in thinking) is in some degree true."

Other facts about pipe smokers surfaced in 1971, in a Time Research Report.[3] This survey of pipe smokers was based on 1,796 completed questionnaires. Of those surveyed, over three-quarters were married, about thirty-six years old, and "upscale" in income, education, and occupation. Of those under thirty-five, 64 percent were college-educated. The large majority of those questioned said that they began smoking a pipe because of the taste; others chose the pipe for reasons of health, economy, relaxation, aroma, or approval of women.

That "approval of women" could be a factor in taking up pipe smoking emphasizes the traditional masculine image projected by the pipe smoker. It would seem to indicate that the great majority of tobacco users, namely cigarette smokers, do not—despite decades of advertising that portrays he-man cigarette smokers—evoke the same masculine image as pipe smokers.

The traditional image of the pipe smoker is not unlike the special version of masculinity depicted by John Wayne in over a hundred films. Though not to everyone's liking, Wayne displayed some very traditional male traits such as silence, reliability, practicality, unshakeability, strength, and lack of anxiety. These are the qualities of a survivor, a man who can be counted on to endure rough times.

To smoke out the real image of the pipe smoker, however, we need to answer three questions. First, what precisely is this social image of the pipe smoker? Second, do pipe smokers as a group identify with this social image? Third, how do females view pipe smokers? All three of these questions were designed to be answered by the Criswell Survey, which was the first attempt to develop a personality profile of pipe smokers based on their social image.[4]

The initial phases of the Criswell Survey involved individual interviews and group consultations to find out how smokers and nonsmokers saw pipe smokers. In these interviews, people tended to choose certain adjectives to describe their impressions of the pipe smoker: stable, British, very masculine, deliberate, calm, pensive, likes to fiddle with things, selfish, tweedy, older man, distinguished, bearded, collegiate, professorial, staid, not agitated, aloof, internalized, intelligent, patient, a conservative dresser, wears jackets with patches on the elbows.

These responses, given by all sorts of individuals, indicated that the image projected by pipe smokers was of a particular type of man. When the group consulted was of a specific type, the adjectives were also specific. For example, one surveyed group of males and females, none of whom were pipe smokers, gave the following descriptions of a pipe smokers: he has dark straight hair; doesn't talk much; is a professor in a small liberal arts college; is tactile, absentminded, and deep thinking. They also felt that corporations would not hire his type because he is too methodical, slow, and reflective. Now this is very specific indeed.

It was from such interviews that Criswell assembled a checklist of 104 adjectives describing the pipe smoker. This checklist was sent to one thousand pipe smoking males and to one thousand women who knew pipe smokers. The rate of response to the survey was surprisingly high: 397 males (39.7 percent) and 363 females (36.3 percent) returned the questionnaire. They were from all occupational levels and socioeconomic circumstances; married and single; from urban, suburban, and rural backgrounds; and randomly selected from all geographical regions of the United States.

The Criswell Survey made it possible for the first time to delineate scientifically the established social image of pipe smokers. One interesting result was the remarkable consistency with which certain adjectives were chosen to describe the personality of the pipe smoker; the social image was even richer and more precise than might be expected. Another fascinating result was the discovery of certain remarkable inconsistencies. Namely, women saw certain traits in pipe smokers that the smokers themselves did not necessarily see. Women agreed with men that certain traits were typical of pipe smokers, but they used a word the men didn't think of: sexy.

3

BEHIND THE SMOKESCREEN: THE SOCIAL IMAGE OF THE PIPE SMOKER

Your true smoker — he that keeps his pipe in, I mean; and that is the mark by which you may know the true from the sham smoker — your true smoker is a pattern man for consistency. He takes his time about things. You ask his opinion: he thinks twice before he answers once — keeping his pipe in. You offer him a bargain: he considers well before he accepts it — keeping his pipe in. Some ill-natured, quarrelsome fellow tries to provoke him; but he is slow to be provoked — he keeps his pipe in.

     — *Thomas Cooper,* Adam Hornbook

The Criswell Survey revealed that the social image of the pipe smoker is remarkably masculine. Over 90 percent of those surveyed, both men and women, agreed that a pipe smoker is stable, capable, mature, intelligent, dependable, kind, responsible, loyal, sincere, sure, masculine, reliable, good-natured, friendly, solid, strong, conscientious, self-controlled, careful, efficient, logical, gentle, confident, considerate, alert, understanding, realistic, cooperative, thorough, affectionate, attractive, self-confident, practical, industrious, deep-thinking, dignified, and adaptable.

Just as surprising was the consensus as to what pipe smokers were *not*. Both men and women agreed that pipe smokers could not be described as excitable, anxious, flirtatious, shy, impulsive, aloof, restless, nervous, slow, absent-minded, conceited, arrogant, sloppy, or selfish. That there is such a high percentage of agreement on the pipe smoker as *not* shy, aloof, slow, or absent-minded is curious, because these four adjectives might well be thought to be part of the traditional image of pipe smokers. Both in fiction and in film there have been pipe smokers depicted as absent-minded and slow — Dr. Watson was as much a pipe smoker as was Sherlock Holmes. Certainly, there have been pipe smoking men who appear aloof. The very image of General Douglas MacArthur was that of a pipe smoker proud and above it all. But as striking as all this is, the Criswell Survey reveals even more about how male pipe smokers choose to describe themselves.

When the survey asked the men to describe their perceptions of *other* pipe smokers, over 95 percent of male pipe smokers saw their fellows as stable, dependable, kind, capable, responsible, intelligent, and mature. This evidence of the positive regard in which pipe smokers hold one another helps explain the hail-fellow-well-met attitude that they display upon meeting one another, or in exchanging letters of information. The Universal Coterie of Pipe Smokers is the whimsical name given to an informal group of pipe lovers who receive a quarterly newsletter called *The Pipe Smoker's Ephemeris.*[5] It consists almost entirely of letters from smokers the world over telling of new discoveries they have made in pipes or tobaccos, unusual pipe shops in Holland or London, pipe museums in Germany or Denmark, new manufacturers of pipes, and poems, sayings, lore, encomiums and books about pipes, both recent and ancient. The writers are eager to share what they know, and every published letter happily assumes that any genuine pipe smoker is, by that very fact, a marvelous, superior human being and the salt of the earth.

Not only did the Criswell Survey define the social image of pipe smokers as overwhelmingly and traditionally masculine, it also showed that women who know pipe smokers agree with this view and have some very special insights of their own.

About 96 percent of women surveyed described the male pipe smoker first as "mature." Next, they saw him as intelligent, capable, attractive, loyal, masculine, sincere, stable, dependable, kind, friendly, and responsible. If we compare the top ten adjectives of the general list with the top ten of the women's list, we notice that the ladies include three adjectives of their own: attractive, loyal, and masculine. That male pipe smokers did not necessarily see themselves in these terms is, perhaps, evidence of a certain group modesty. Moreover, it tends to underline the survey's finding that pipe smokers were not flirtatious, conceited, or arrogant.

In addition, over 90 percent of the women picked twenty-two other adjectives whose rank order shows the subtle differences between their views and these expressed by both sexes. Women felt that pipe smokers were also strong, solid, reliable, good-natured, sure, self-controlled, gentle, efficient, handsome, conscientious, considerate, logical, confident, cooperative, careful, affectionate, alert, thorough, dignified, understanding, practical, and realistic. The women respondents also agreed that their wondeful pipe smoking acquaintances were not at all shy, aloof, slow or absent-minded. So it appears that we can strike these adjectives from our supposed traditional image of pipe smokers.

But we should notice further contrasts between the men's and women's views. Ninety percent of the women included adjectives that were not in the men's 90-percent list. These were: attractive, gentle, loyal, masculine, sincere, friendly, affectionate, and dignified. A computer analysis of the Criswell Survey revealed that 11.3 percent more females than males described the pipe smoker as attractive; 17.7 percent more females than males described the pipe smoker as handsome; and last, but certainly not least, 14.3 percent more females than males described the pipe smoker as sexy. This is an anomaly over which male pipe smokers will probably not disagree. More and more, the pipe smoker is beginning to look like the ideal choice as lover and as husband. Unquestionably, the Criswell Survey, were it better known, would send thousands of males to their local tobacconist, seeking to transform themselves into resplendent and female-pleasing pipe smokers.

A Californian, reading of these findings, wrote the following:

> I myself, as a pipe smoker, coincide with your finding in the respects that I have an extremely high IQ, am a member of Mensa, and am sexy, having fought a life-long affliction of satyriasis (the male equivalent of nymphomania, as you know). But on the other hand, rather than "stable," I am highly unstable, emotionally, contrary to your findings. In reflecting on why I smoke a pipe I must say with malice aforethought that I have, since a small child, been aware that women freak out over pipe smokers; so therefore to diminish the frustration of the satyriasis I smoked a pipe. It opened the door, so to speak — the females never suspecting the Real Me and my True Motives that lay behind the pipe smoking. Aromatic tobaccos, which I hate, I use in furtherance of My Real Goal.

This is only one response of a pipe smoker to the Criswell Survey. To underline this discovery of the sexy pipe smoker, here is a letter from a somewhat more mature appreciator of both pipes and women:

> To assist the statistics of your research I submit myself as a statistic in confirmation of your conclusion. I am 67, and to my surprise I have never been in a better sex condition in my life. I am a pipe smoker. Of course now being fortified with the knowledge that pipe smokers are terrifically better than nervous cigarette smokers with the appreciation of the presence of ladies in mind, I shall enjoy each pipeful of tobacco in a most glorious manner, even perhaps to the point that I might smirk at myself each time I light a pipe.

Do all of these virtues really come from smoking a pipe? Is it simply a question of buying a pipe and some tobacco and then

Figure 2. Chinese Water Pipe. Arab and Indian traders introduced the water pipe to the Chinese. However, they preferred something less cumbersome than the *nargeeleh* and the *hookah,* so they miniaturized them into a portable, all-metal pipe. The Chinese water pipe usually had two special features: a tobacco box was built into the pipe and it could be fitted with two bowls: one for tobaccos, one for opium.

puffing oneself to perfection? Or is it that certain men — those who are pleasure-seeking, mellow, ripe of judgment, and warm of feelings — are automatically drawn to smoke a pipe? (Of course, it may be a combination of the two.) Whichever it may be, we have a clearly established social image of the pipe smoker of the most positive kind. To what degree pipe smokers actually fit this image is a question we will consider further in Chapters 4, 5, and 6.

4

THE PERSONALITY OF THE
PIPE SMOKER:
EXTRAVERT OR INTROVERT?

The fact is, squire, the moment a man takes to a pipe he becomes a philosifer; it's a poor man's friend; it calms the mind, soothes the temper, and makes a man patient under troubles. It has made more good men, good husbands, kind masters, indulgent fathers and honest fellows, than any other blessed thing in this universal world.

— *Thomas Haliburton,* The Clockmaker

What type of person are you? This question about personality types is as old as the human race, and it reflects the universal human concern to understand why some people think, behave, and react in one way and others think, behave, and react in quite different ways. When we say that "birds of a feather flock together" or that "like attracts like," we are, whether we know it or not, attempting to classify human beings according to the typical ways in which they think, behave, and react.

One of the oldest methods of personality classification was that of the Greek physician, Galen, who in the second century A.D. wrote that human beings fell into four types: melancholic, phlegmatic, sanguine, and choleric. For centuries, these terms were used to describe certain kinds of persons.

Other classifications, such as in astrology, derive from the position of the celestial constellations at the time of a person's birth. "Look out for him, he's a Scorpio," or "That's typical of the way a Gemini behaves," are astrological classifications that have become part of our popular culture. Some people believe that the shape of a person's body tells us what kind of personality that individual tends toward. For example, endomorphic persons with soft, round bodies are supposed to be relaxed, comfortable, sociable types; mesomorphic persons with husky, rectangular bodies are thought to be energetic, assertive, and power loving; and ectomorphic persons with linear, fragile bodies are presumed to be restrained and solitary.

Today, one of the most commonly accepted ways of describing personality types is based on Jung's distinction between extraverts and introverts. An extravert is "turned outward"; an introvert is "turned inward." Thus the consciousness of a person is either focused outward upon the things of this world, or it is focused inward upon the person himself.

"Extravert" and "introvert" have become such household words that few people realize they were the invention of the famous Swiss psychologist, Carl Jung. As Jung explains it, the extravert is primarily motivated by the external situation. His consciousness is attuned to objective events and his thoughts, behavior, and reactions are determined by them. According to Jung, "If a man thinks, feels, acts and actually lives in a way that is *directly* correlated with the objective conditions and their demands, he is extraverted. His life makes it perfectly clear that it is the object and not his subjective view that plays the determining role in his consciousness."[6]

Introverts are quite different. When they look at things, they are conscious of something that the extravert doesn't see. For the introvert, the importance of what he sees depends on the way it affects him personally. He is more reflective than the extravert, and attempts to understand everything he sees. The introvert is not overpowered by his objective surroundings. Instead, his interest in self-knowledge serves to buffer him from the outside world. His reactions are slower and more thoughtful; he is not easily provoked. His self-interest gives him a certain stability. Jung says that "the tendency of the introvert is to defend himself against all demands from outside, to conserve his energy by withdrawing it from objects, thereby consolidating his own position."[7]

At the beginning of Chapter 2 we asked two sets of questions: "Do I prefer action to planning for action? Would I rate myself as a lively individual? Do I usually take the initiative in making new friends?" If you say yes to this set of questions, you are placing yourself in the category of the extravert. The other set described the introvert: "Do I become so absorbed in whatever I'm doing that I don't like to be interrupted and have to change to something new? Do I feel I can really enjoy myself with friends when I've done my duty and finished whatever task I've had in mind? Do I remain outwardly calm when people around me are disturbed and excited?"

It is evident that the type of person described by psychologists as an introvert is remarkably similar to the type of person described by the Criswell Survey as a pipe smoker. This masculine minority that stands apart from the rest of society is characterized by much more than carrying a pipe and a pouch full of tobacco; pipe smokers seem to have a certain psychological makeup of which smoking a pipe is an expression.

It is not easy being an introvert. As a child the introvert is not outgoing, quick-acting, or sociable. He may prefer a good book to a good baseball game, and thus be considered aloof, retiring, and shy. In school the introvert absorbs things slowly and carefully, not showing off his knowledge until he is certain of what he has learned.

The extravert, on the other hand, is much more successful in handling his external situation. He quickly learns how to gain the approval of others, and he reaps the rewards of this social acceptance. As an adult, the extravert excels in the professions that require public approval; the politician, the public relations person, the salesman, and the hustler have a sharp eye for what the public wants, and they are amply rewarded. This is quite different from the diminished social approval accorded to the introverted professions; teachers, writers, researchers, composers, and painters are rarely recompensed sufficiently for their contributions to society.

The introvert and extravert "are so different and present such a striking contrast," observes Jung, "that their existence becomes quite obvious even to the layman once it has been pointed out. Everyone knows those reserved, inscrutable, rather shy people who form the strongest possible contrast to the open, sociable, jovial, or at least friendly and approachable characters who are on good terms with everybody, or quarrel with everybody, but always relate to them in some way and in turn are affected by them."[8]

These two psychological types are found in all cultures and in all social classes. They cut across the lines of education and sex. They are, according to Jung, the two basic tendencies for personality formation throughout the human race. Something that is so universal in human society cannot be arbitrary; Jung concludes that it must rest upon a biological foundation.

Turning outward *to* the objective world, or turning inward *away* from the objective world are two forms of biological adaptation. Jung observes that some animals (like flies and rabbits) preserve their species by having a great amount of offspring. Their powers of defense, however, are not good, and their lifespans are short. Other species, such as lions and wolves, which are equipped with adequate means of self-preservation, have a low fertility rate and a relatively longer lifespan. Jung sums it up:

> This biological difference, it seems to me, is not merely analogous to, but the actual foundation of, our two psychological modes of adaptation. I must content myself with this broad hint. It is sufficient to note that the peculiar nature of the extravert constantly

Figure 3. Alsatian Porcelain Pipe. This spectacular pipe is a favorite among Germanic peoples. The porcelain bowl is fitted to a bulbous chamber which catches tars and moisture. The long stem is of cherrywood and the bit usually of horn. The long air chamber gives a cool smoke, but the beautifully decorated bowl so heats up that its surface inevitably cracks into tiny fissures.

urges him to expend and propagate himself in every way, while the tendency of the introvert is to defend himself against all demands from outside, to conserve his energy by withdrawing it from objects, thereby consolidating his own position.[9]

So Jung believed that the contrasts between extravert and introvert are rooted in profound biological differences. And we should particularly notice "the tendency of the introvert to defend himself against all demands from outside." If pipe smokers are introverts and if introverts defend themselves from the external world, is it then possible that the pipe smoker, unconsciously but certainly, chooses to smoke a pipe in order to "defend" himself?

Everything points to a biological motivation for pipe smoking. What we need is the link between knowing scientifically that certain types of men smoke pipes and knowing scientifically *why* certain types of men smoke pipes. As we will see in the next chapter, thanks to German-English psychologist H. J. Eysenck, we have that link.

5

BEHIND THE IMAGE:
A HEALTHY INTROVERT

After I started smoking a pipe, I lost all desire to smoke cigars, regardless of make or cost. I now smoke one of my many pipes after each meal and sometimes more often. It gives me great satisfaction, and without my "smokes" the day would not be complete.

Of course I never inhale. I will be seventy years of age my next birthday, and although I cannot give credit to my pipe for continued good health, I feel that it will keep me going for many years in the future.

— A Texas pipe smoker

During each twenty-four-hour cycle of our lives we alternate between sleeping and wakefulness, a steady rhythm that is the pulse of life itself. All living things share this rhythm; it is life's response to night and day, winter and summer, the oscillations of the earth as it whirls before the energizing rays of the sun.

How deeply we sleep and how active we are when awake are relative matters, which vary from day to day for each individual. But each of us has a typical, long-term pattern of sleep and wakefulness. Some individuals sleep deeper and longer than others; some individuals are more vividly awake and for longer periods than others. If we were to draw an absolute scale showing the degrees of sleep and wakefulness that humans are capable of, it would be something like this:

> Manic
> Very Alert
> Alert
> Awake
> Drowsy
> Hypnogogic/Hypnopompic
> Sleep
> Rapid Eye Movement Sleep
> Coma

Psychologists speak of these as "levels of arousal," by which they mean the level of activity of the entire body, particularly the central nervous system. Some of us attain our maximum level of arousal in the early part of the day, while others of us don't really get the cobwebs out of our heads until the afternoon. Still others are night people, fully awake after the rest of us have gone to sleep.

Another way to describe our levels of arousal is to focus on the amount of stimulation that our bodies normally undergo. Some people need very little stimulation, or they may need it only in gradual increments. Other people may either need a lot of stimulation all the time, or only at certain times of the day. For example, some people wince when they hear loud music in the morning, while others love it. There are those who prefer their greatest stimulation in the evening, perhaps to the distress of the early risers who, by then, can tolerate only silence.

Whatever our differences of arousal, all of us need stimulation of varying degrees and duration. And, happily, we don't have to look for stimulation: it is all around us. We are surrounded by an ocean of stimulation—electrical, mechanical, chemical, acoustical, photic, electromagnetic. These energies bombard us constantly, and the degree to which we are aroused depends in large part on how many of these energies we allow to stimulate us.

If we were suddenly deprived of sensual stimulation, we would soon discover just how dependent we are on it. Experiments in "sensory deprivation" have shown that if humans are placed in an isolation tank or a dark, quiet place, they eventually become confused and deranged both in their perceptions and their judgment. Deprived of incoming sensations, the human spirit and body eventually suffocate; an unstimulating environment is anathema to life itself.

So, in varying degrees, we need outside stimulation and our bodies use as much of this stimulation as they are able to handle. When the energies around us strike the surface of our bodies, the body's sensory receptors translate that energy into electrochemical impulses that travel inward on neuronal tracks toward the central nervous system, which in turn channels them along the spine upward to the brain. The brain sorts out these sensory impulses and makes sense of them.

A prime function of one part of the brain is to monitor the amount of sensory stimulation that is allowed to arouse the top of the brain, or cortex. This monitor of stimulation, located beneath the cortex, is called the reticular activating system (RAS). In general terms, the RAS can be seen as a type of threshold through which the ascending sensory stimulation passes. Also in general terms, if one's threshold is high, less stimulation will reach the cortex, and thus there will be less arousal. Conversely, if the threshold is low, a great deal of arousal will take place.

Since we know that some persons receive more stimulation than others, this tells us that people vary according to how much stimulation their RAS allows to impinge upon the cerebral cortex. These relative differences in the threshold of the RAS go far to explain why some of us are "morning people" and others "night people," as well as the reasons for the differences between stimulus-seekers and stimulus-avoiders.

It also sheds light on the difference between people whom psychologists have termed "sharpeners" and "levelers." It has been noticed in experimental studies that, if asked to draw a certain angular shape from memory, some people will draw the angle sharper than the original; others will flatten out the angle. Those who exaggerate the angle have the cognitive style of the sharpener, and this tendency toward exaggeration will show itself in other things they do, whether it be in embellishing a story or in the degree of enthusiasm with which they respond to something. The leveler, on the other hand, tends to play down and soften his response. The sharpener may say, "Oh, it was the most amazing thing!" The leveler, describing the same experience, may say, "Oh, it was really nothing."

What is important here is that research has shown that the sharpener *needs* to exaggerate things and make them more stimulating, while the leveler has just the opposite need: to tone things down so that they are not too stimulating. Psychological studies that relate these two cognitive styles to extraverted and introverted personalities have found that the extravert tends to be the sharpener and the introvert is usually a leveler.

H. J. Eysenck, a psychologist at the University of London, has done an enormous amount of research on the physiological differences that underlie the distinctions between extraverts and introverts. He and his colleagues have come to the conclusion that the differences between extraverts and introverts are due in large measure to differences in arousability. Eysenck takes the position that "extraverts may be characterized by low cortical arousal levels, introverts by high cortical arousal levels . . . these differences might be caused in turn by differential threshold levels in the reticular formation, whose main function is of course the control of arousal (and inhibition) levels in the cortex."[10]

This is a fascinating discovery, for it says that extraverted persons have low cortical arousal, which in turn explains why they are driven to seek outward stimulation and exaggeration in order to function normally. In the same fashion, this informs us that introverts *already* have high cortical arousal levels, and thus "defend" themselves from external stimulation, leveling out things in order to function normally. Extraverts are outward-turning stimulus-seekers; introverts are inward-turning stimulus-avoiders.

What is surprising about this is that Eysenck's research makes it clear that the introvert is experiencing just the reverse of what might be popularly thought, for the introvert avoids and defends himself against external stimulation for a very important reason: *he has too much stimulation already.* The quiet and retiring behavior of the introvert is a way of diminishing his already high level of cortical arousal so that he can function at an optimal level. The introvert seeks ways of "coming down." The extravert, however, is in the opposite situation. Constitutionally he has a low level of cortical arousal, so in order to function optimally he needs to "get himself up" by seeking stimulation. For each, their behavior is a way of correcting their neurophysiological constitution, so that they can feel and function normally.

Eysenck and others have produced voluminous evidence for this theory, which so well helps us understand why introverts and extraverts behave as they do. Each is seeking a balance; each is attempting to do the things that make his system function best. One type of personality is not "better" than the other; both are compensating for the bias that is built into their own brain systems. The introvert has to avoid excess stimulation, just as the extravert has to seek it.

How this relates to pipe smoking would be only circumstantial, except for the fact that Eysenck in his many studies of the variables of extraversion-introversion also turned his attention to the use of tobacco by these two personality types. He discovered at least three very useful facts:

First, nicotine is not equally stimulating to all human beings. In some persons it leads to stimulation and arousal; in others it leads in the opposite direction.

> We would suggest that the effects of nicotine depend on the degree
> of arousal in the cortex; when arousal is high, the effects are de-
> pressing, whereas when arousal is low, the effects are stimulating.
> The degree of arousal is primarily a function of two factors: (a) the
> personality of the subject (primarily his position on the extraver-
> sion-introversion continuum); and (b) the conditions obtaining at
> the time, i.e., external determinants of arousal such as the degree
> of sensory stimulation, etc. [11]

Second, the use of tobacco is a way of controlling one's internal
state of arousal. That is, "Introverts should more frequently use
nicotine for tranquilizing purposes, extraverts for stimulating purposes."

Third, Eysenck's research has further shown that cigarette smokers
tend to be extraverts, seeking arousal, and that pipe smokers tend to
be introverts, seeking to reduce arousal.

It now becomes understandable why it is that the stable, capable,
mature pipe smokers are as they are, and why through the years they
have created a social image that is so clear and consistent. Pipe
smokers tend to be introverts with a high degree of wakefulness and
arousal, so high in fact that ritualistic puffing on the tobacco pipe
calms them and renders their lives more efficient and comfortable.
The stability of their social image rests upon their neurophysiology.
That is why their character traits are so predictable.

Eysenck has, by the way, added one more interesting observation
about introverts and extraverts. He has cross-correlated two other
factors with extraversion-introversion — the factor of stability/in-
stability (See Figure 4).

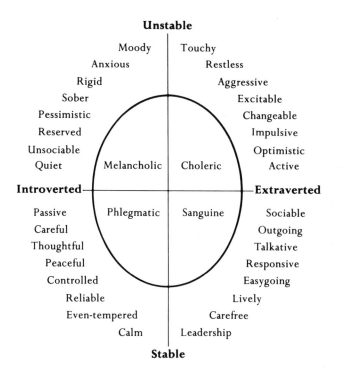

Figure 4.

Notice that the adjectives on the side of introversion and on the side of stable roughly coincide with the adjectives used to describe pipe smokers in those responding to the Criswell Survey.

As if pipe smokers did not already have enough to be smug about in their social image! The introverted lovers of the joys of the pipe are not only highly awake, but it appears that they are also highly stable.

PART II

WHAT THE
BODY SAYS

6

AROUSAL

Motto for A Tobacco Jar

Come! don't refuse sweet Nicotina's aid,
But woo the goddess through a yard of clay;
And soon you'll own she is the fairest maid
To stifle pain, and drive old Care away.
Nor deem it waste, what though to ash she burns,
If for your outlay you get good returns!

—Anonymous, nineteenth century

*T*he singular reputation enjoyed by pipe smokers is due to the fact that they are singular men: stable introverts who remain cool while others lose their heads. Although there may be a number of pipe smokers who do not fit this role, scientific research indicates most do.

The pipe smoker lives his life differently. He has a distinctive way of meeting the hour-to-hour, day-to-day events and challenges of life. He has a certain way of handling himself and keeping his balance. As an introvert, he may have a limited tolerance for external stimulation, but he is not merely passive in this respect. There are actions he can take to keep himself in balance.

What the pipe smoker keeps in balance is the level of arousal of his entire body. A certain degree of arousal is necessary in all human beings, because this alertness is needed to meet the challenges of the world. Some situations require much alertness, others less. A man who is slated to make an all-important speech to a large audience discovers that he is far too keyed up, so much so that he is likely to botch the whole affair. So, half an hour before his presentation, he strolls out of the auditorium. There, all alone, he looks at the evening sky and breathes in deeply the tranquil night air. After twenty minutes, he returns to the auditorium feeling composed and balanced, ready to do his best. This is one way of controlling the degree of arousal.

If the second-string quarterback has been sitting on the bench during three quarters of the football game and is alerted by the coach that he will soon be going in, what does he do? He gets up and runs up and down the sidelines a bit and then begins receiving the ball from the center and practicing short passes. He must "get himself up" to the level of arousal that is needed for maximum efficiency when he enters the game. This is an opposite manner of controlling the degree of one's arousal.

Both the speaker and the quarterback are doing the same thing: trying to establish the optimal condition of arousal for the task that must be done. Psychologists refer to a "U-shaped" relationship between arousal and optimal efficiency. This means that we can do something efficiently only if we are in an appropriate state of arousal—too much arousal and we become inefficient, too little arousal and we also become inefficient. So everybody seeks the state of arousal that is just right, a golden mean.

Arousal may be a vague term to describe what we are feeling, but to physiological psychologists it is very precise. Our nervous systems tend in one of two directions: one is a state of rest, recuperation, and tissue building (called the parasympathetic state), and the other is a state of arousal, when the whole system readies itself for a struggle or for a retreat from a danger. This is commonly called the "fight or flight" arousal of the sympathetic state of the nervous system. When a challenge or threat is at hand, the sympathetic state dominates; when the need for rest or recuperation is at hand, the parasympathetic state dominates. It is by the activation of one or the other of these two states that humans unconsciously control their level of arousal.

Other bodily changes occur when the sympathetic nervous system takes over. For example, when we are keyed up, the pupil of the eye dilates and the retina goes through a photochemical change that lets in more light. This readies the visual system for action. Muscles of the neck also turn the head quickly toward visual and aural stimuli. You have probably noticed that animals, when aroused, prick up their ears and automatically flare their nostrils to sniff the air.

In this state, the muscles of the body show greater electrical activity and their degree of tightness increases, readying the entire body for action. The blood vessels in the limbs contract and those in the head expand; this sends more blood and oxygen to the brain, promoting mental acuity. The aroused sympathetic nervous state also changes the frequency of our brain waves: the electrical frequency, when measured by an electroencephalographic machine, increases and becomes more excited. These factors, along with changes in breathing, heart rate, blood pressure, and in other bodily functions, make it clear that the whole body is involved in the arousal state. Even though it is virtually unconscious, it is a powerful and comprehensive change in the entire physical being.

From what we already know about the social image of pipe smokers and their general tendency toward introversion, we would expect that in the course of packing, lighting, and puffing a pipe the pipe smoker diminishes his normally high state of arousal and alertness. In pilot studies made by the authors, this was in fact found to be the case. In EEG brain wave measurements (which are at this stage giving suggestive rather than conclusive results) it was found that pipe smokers showed brain waves that steadily held at the calm and balanced alpha level (eight to twelve cycles per second) while they were smoking. On similar tests made with cigarette smokers, the brain-wave frequency moved up and down in an unstable and excitable manner. The cigarette seemed to agitate the smoker, while the pipe appeared to calm him.

All of these matters are important if we are to understand the very real physiological and psychological significance of smoking cigarettes or pipes. Both are ways of controlling (sometimes consciously, most of the time unconsciously) the general state of bodily arousal in order to be at an optimal state of efficiency. This scientific information also suggests why introverted and stable pipe smokers remain cool while others lose their heads: they are most efficient when they are most relaxed.

7

THE PIPE OF PEACE: RELAXATION

Now, the pipe calms a man; it slackens his pulse, lulls his restlessness, lays unruly haste and anxiety to sleep, and makes a man willing to stay in the armchair and enjoy it as one of the pleasantest and most comfortable things in life, and let the world, if it will, go a-gadding.

Thomas Cooper, Adam Hornbook

Until recently, it was thought that people became ill for one of three reasons: they had accidents, they had infections, or they simply wore out. But now we know that there is another reason for human maladies: stress. Recent medical research, particularly the work done by Dr. Hans Selye, has made it certain that stress is a major cause of physical and mental illnesses.

Stress is any condition that adds pressure or strain to our lives, forcing us to adjust and adapt. How long it lasts and how strong it is are relative matters, as are our ways of handling it and the degree to which it bothers us.

During the latter half of the twentieth century, it has become the common lot of mankind to live under a considerable burden of stress. It is for this reason, most probably, that this factor was only recently brought forward by medical science. We have learned that stress can kill and that stress can maim, and its cumulative effects may lead to some of the most commonly known health problems of our age: heart attacks, strokes, cardiovascular blockage, respiratory failures, and more.

It is not simply the physical aspects of overwork and physical exhaustion that are behind these stress-originated illnesses. The psychological aspects are much more significant. To listen to a news broadcast or to read a newspaper is to be compelled to think and react to calamity, catastrophe, and possible doom. But the stress of life typical of contemporary society is also tied to the way we lead our lives. All too often we live in states of constant suspense, expectation, and tension. Individuals, corporations, national governments are all goal-oriented. This means that we live obligated to the future, to the next day, the next week. Tomorrow we must do this, so that the next day we can do that, and we must worry about it today so that it will be done tomorrow. When one problem or goal is taken care of, it is immediately replaced with another. Thus we can rarely be satisfied with "a job well done," because it never *is* done.

These are the things that constitute the stress of life in contemporary society, leading to bad backs, bad hearts, bad breath, and bad dispositions. Yet all of these maladies are unnecessary and avoidable. **The dire effects of stress can be prevented very simply by relaxing.**

Stress has little chance of accumulating if humans will stop from time to time during the day and put both mind and body completely out of gear through relaxation. Because we know that mental and physical tensions build up daily, we know that regular relief from these tensions will leave us free from the unhealthy effects of stress. The popularity during the 1970s of meditation was not necessarily the sign of a new *religious* consciousness, but was more likely the sign of *health* consciousness.

Not surprisingly, such systems as Transcendental Meditation are quite vocal in advertising the health benefits of meditative practice. And, apart from meditation, there are other ways in which we can achieve relaxation. The act of deep breathing is one; another is lying on one's back, arms and legs slightly spread in the "corpse pose" of

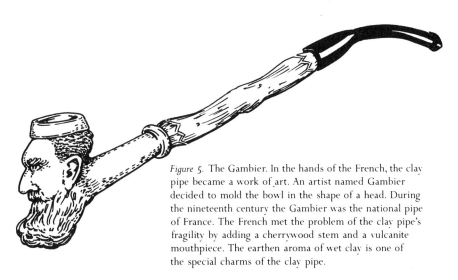

Figure 5. The Gambier. In the hands of the French, the clay pipe became a work of art. An artist named Gambier decided to mold the bowl in the shape of a head. During the nineteenth century the Gambier was the national pipe of France. The French met the problem of the clay pipe's fragility by adding a cherrywood stem and a vulcanite mouthpiece. The earthen aroma of wet clay is one of the special charms of the clay pipe.

hatha yoga. The procedure called "progressive relaxation" will do the trick, as will self-hypnosis. A good twenty-minute walk will also relax the body. And the many different forms of biofeedback are known to be effective ways of relaxing.

Another excellent way of relaxing is to smoke a pipe. Indeed, pipe smoking is an extraordinarily effective (and socially acceptable) way of stopping what one is doing, taking time out, and focusing on sensual pleasures. Pipe smoking creates a personal space and lets us momentarily stand aside from life's other commitments.

Most important of all, pipe smoking is an effective way of triggering the dominance of the parasympathetic nervous system, which brings physiological relaxation, rest, recuperation, and repair of tissues. In our discussion of arousal, we dealt with the "fight or flight" excitement of the sympathetic nervous system, but when we turn our attention to relaxation, we are dealing with the tranquilized calmness of the parasympathetic nervous system.

We have already discovered that the social image of a pipe smoker is that he is calm, easygoing, and contemplative in comparison with other men. We have seen that this is a result of the effects of pipe smoking on the parasympathetic system. We know that pipe smokers are more relaxed because their personalities tend to lead them toward relaxation and the reduction of arousal. Defending themselves against stimulation from the outside world is characteristic of pipe smokers. They don't need arousal. Before he reads the newspaper, before he tenses up in anticipation of future goals, before he is caught in the ethos of progress and production, the pipe smoker has already been reducing his stress, arousal and excitation.

Hundreds of years before stress was discovered, pipe smokers discovered the secret of relaxation. Before there was talk of TM, progressive relaxation, biofeedback, and all the rest, there was pipe smoking. It is one of the most venerable traditions of stress-reduction known to mankind and was practiced enthusiastically by primitive societies long before French and English explorers found North American Indians smoking their calumets in rituals of great peace.

The very act of stopping one's regular activities to take out a pipe is a further spur to relaxation. Sniffing the pipe, checking it for ash or dottle, cleaning the stem, taking out the pouch and sniffing the contents, dipping the fingers into the tobacco and scooping small amounts bit by bit into the pipe's bowl, packing and smoothing the tobacco, lighting the pipe from the center out to the periphery, puffing the pipe lightly while tamping down the first rising bits of ash, and then settling into the slow, rhythmic, euphoric experience of little puffs inward and outward, the smoke curling up and out into the atmosphere, wreaths of it arching up to the nose, so that one rhythmically and pulsatingly enjoys the heady odor of the tobacco as well as the taste—all of this extraordinary ritual amounts to self-hypnotism. The pipe smoker is happily and ineluctibly drawn into peace and calmness.

The self-induced mesmerism of pipe smoking has been recounted over and again in the hundreds of poems and anecdotes written in praise of the soothing effects of the pipe. Richard Le Gallienne celebrated the relaxation of a good pipe in this poem:

> With Pipe and Book at the close of day.
> O! what is sweeter, mortal, say!
> It matters not what book on knee,
> Old Izaak or the Odyssey.
>
> And though one's eyes will dream astray,
> And lips forget to sue or sway,
> It is "enough to merely Be,"
> With Pipe and Book.
>
> What though our modern skies be grey,
> As bards aver, I will not pray
> For "soothing Death" to succor me,
> But ask thus much, O! Fate, of thee,
> A little longer yet to stay
> With Pipe and Book.

Clearly there is no question in Le Gallienne's mind as to the relaxing qualities of pipe smoking, nor is there in this anecdote taken from a novel of Edward Bulwer, *Night and Morning*, written in 1851:

"A very warm even, sir," said a passenger seated at his right; puffing while he spoke, from a short German pipe, a volume of smoke into Philip's face.

"Very warm. Be so good as to smoke into the face of the gentle-man on the other side of you," returned Philip petulantly.

"Ho, Ho!" replied the passenger, with a loud, powerful laugh — the laugh of a strong man. "You don't take to the pipe yet; you will by and by, when you have known the cares and anxieties that I have gone through. A pipe! — it is a great soother, a pleasant comforter! Blue devils fly before its honest breath! It ripens the brain — it opens the heart; and the man who smokes, thinks like a sage and acts like a Samaritan!

This great soother and pleasant comforter is powerful indeed (even inspiring traces of rudeness)! Such extravagant praise is normally reserved for man's enthusiasm for womanhood and the loving solace of femininity. As we will see, the solace of the pipe is not unrelated to the solace of the female. In fact, one seems to lead easily to the other.

8

WHERE THERE'S SMOKE THERE'S FIRE:
SEX AND THE PIPE SMOKER

Memories

The lamplight seems to glimmer with a flicker of surprise,
As I turn it low — to rest me of the dazzle in my eyes,
And light my pipe in silence, save a sigh that seems to yoke
Its fate with my tobacco, and to vanish with the smoke.

A face of lily beauty, with a form of airy grace,
Floats out of my tobacco as the "Genii" from the vase;
And I thrill beneath the glances of a pair of azure eyes,
As glowing as the summer and as tender as the skies.

—*James Whitcomb Riley,* An Old Sweetheart of Mine

*T*he American Indians have always held that tobacco is a healing
and health-giving herb. When the pipe and tobacco were introduced into Europe in the sixteenth century, the various medical benefits claimed for it so expanded the reputation of tobacco that it was
almost instantly seized upon as the great and universal panacea.

This great cure-all was not only inhaled, it was also to be eaten,
sniffed, taken in pills, applied to the body as a poultice, and rubbed
on the body as a linament. It was good for hiccoughs and it was good
for imbecility. It cured earaches and dysentery, syphilis and corpu-
lence, carbuncles and the plague. Jean Nicot, ambassador from the

French court of Catherine de Medici, sent his queen some tobacco as a cure for her habitual headaches. The remedy was so successful that she officially named the healing weed *Nicotiana* in honor of her benefactor, hence the word "nicotine."

In the seventeenth century, some physicians prescribed tobacco as a cure for impotence, while others encouraged husbands to induce their wives to use it as an aid to procreation and the spawning of healthy children.

There were, of course, others—from King James I on down—who vehemently decried the use of the "stinking weed" as a sure corruption of body, spirit, and soul. James believed that the introduction of tobacco essence into the bowels as an enema was its sole medicinal use, and he so used it via clyster-pipe for colonic disorders.

But eventually the excessive claims, pro and con, canceled one another out, and the health-giving uses of tobacco gave way to its pleasure-giving uses. Pleasure, needless to say, takes countless different forms. There are many pleasures and many satisfactions, intellectual, moral, and physical, but the pleasure and satisfaction of pipe smoking is heavily sensual.

Indeed, pipe smoking is a feast of sensuality. The moisture of the tobacco, the shape of the pipe, the texture of the surface, and the heat of the bowl all speak to the sense of touch. The design and color of the pipe, the changing hue of the burning leaf, the off-and-on glow of the orange fire, and the curling wreaths of smoke arching into space constitute a visual satisfaction enjoyed by all pipe smokers. The smell of fresh tobacco in the canister, the odors of the pipe bowl, and the aroma of the smoke are a cornucopia of olfactory delights. And the taste of the myriad concocted flavors of tobacco—Virginia and Maryland and latakia and cavendish in a thousand mixtures—constitutes a gustatory banquet in which the palate ceaselessly enjoys the flavor of a meal that never fills the stomach. Even the ears are regaled with the sounds of gentle puffing as rhythmic and reassuring as a heartbeat. There are few human experiences, enjoyable in public as well as private, that are as roundly sensual as the smoking of a pipe. The only human activities that can achieve this level of sensuality are a truly great meal and sex.

Which reminds us of the curious fact that, in the Criswell Survey, male pipe smokers responded to the description of themselves as "sexy" 68 percent of the time. But females chose this adjective over 82 percent of the time. This difference becomes compelling when we remember that the women were already personally acquainted with a pipe smoker! Thus we must assume that they were not so much guessing as reporting.

In one computer breakdown of the survey, respondents of both sexes were grouped together under age categories: over thirty, over forty, and over fifty, yielding even more provocative information. These age groups were divided according to whether they thought the adjective "sexy" was most descriptive of the pipe smoker, somewhat descriptive, the least descriptive, or not at all. Here is the breakdown:

Age	Most	Somewhat	Least	Not
over thirty	39.8 percent	42.8 percent	11.0 percent	6.1 percent
over forty	25.0	46.1	16.2	12.7
over fifty	17.3	36.4	24.7	20.4

If we take "most" and "somewhat" responses to be positive, this means that of the under-forty group over 82 percent claimed that the pipe smoker was sexy; of those under fifty years, over 71.1 percent agreed; and of those fifty years and over, 53.7 percent said yes. The positive response of over 82 percent among the under-forty group is impressively large, just as is the 71 percent of the next age group. But what is even more impressive is to learn that in an age group that *began* at fifty and extended all the way to seventy, the positive responses were over 53 percent. Again, remembering that these are pipe smokers and the women who know them — not a random popu-lation — we can assume that the sexy nature of pipe smokers their answers project is the description of a personal reality.

Quite conceivably, there really *is* fire behind this smoke, and when we ask ourselves why, the answer is not hard to discover. The pipe smoker *is* a sensual person because pipe smoking is a sensual pursuit that he enjoys over and over again. And he does not neces-sarily pursue this enjoyment in the confines of his own home; he does it in public for all to see . . . for women to see.

What women see is the patient and skillful manner in which he creates his own sensual enjoyment: the gentleness, the slowness, the attentiveness, the unfeigned delight, the immersion of all the senses in a ritualistic revel that is almost trancelike. And the cornerstone of this sensual absorption — and its justification — is the achievement of relaxation, that is, the dominance of the parasympathetic nervous system.

In their pioneering research on the physiology of human sexual behavior, Masters and Johnson delineated four distinct phases in the cycle of sexual excitement and satisfaction: (1) excitement, (2) plateau, (3) orgasm, and (4) resolution. During the excitement phase of sexual arousal, there is increased heart rate, blood pressure, and muscular tension. Specifically, the genital reactions of the male involve erection of the penis due to vasocongestion in the blood vessels, flattening and elevation of the scrotal sac, and partial eleva-tion of both testes. This initial phase of sexual excitement occurs because of the arousal of the sympathetic nervous system.

But the capacity to go from the initial phase of sexual excite-ment to the plateau phase is nothing less than the ability to switch from the sympathetic to the parasympathetic nervous state. It is this second phase of relaxation that allows the erection to maintain itself, and for rhythmic movements to course through the body's musculature. If the individual is tense and unable to leave the sympa-thetic stage of excitement, either the erection will not maintain

Figure 6. Calabash. The calabash tree grows a large, gourd-like fruit which, when dray, is hollow, lightweight and quite hard. The curled tip-end of the dried gourd is cut off; a stem is inserted into the small end and a ceramic or meerschaum bowl set into the large end. Smoke is drawn from the bowl into the interior chamber of the gourd where it cools a bit before being drawn through the stem. Light to hold and pleasing in shape, the calabash is one of the mellowest of pipes to smoke.

itself or the entire cycle will suddenly abort in premature ejaculation. It is, then, the ability to slide into relaxation and parasympathetic dominance that leads to the culmination of orgasm, which brings on a paroxysm of sympathetic nervous dominance once again, followed by the resolution phase which is a final return to the calmness of parasympathetic dominance.

Thus the cycle of complete sexual satisfaction is a roller coaster ride of rising sympathetic arousal, descending parasympathetic relaxation, followed by even higher sympathetic arousal, and terminated with even deeper parasympathetic relaxation. What this suggests is that the ability to go from initial sexual excitement to full orgasmic satisfaction is utterly dependent upon the capacity to shake off sympathetic dominance and sail along the plateau of relaxation and muscular suppleness.

It just happens that pipe smokers are, by and large, experts in cooling down the sympathetic state. They do it daily. And the implication is that they may very well be experts at riding the roller coaster of sexuality. Not only can they take the stage of initial arousal into a relaxed and easygoing plateau of preorgasmic preparation, but when the final orgasmic peak is past, they happily slip down into mellow sloughs of full postorgasmic calmness. This fourth phase of relaxation is a welcome and expected tranquillity, unlike the arousal-seeking cigarette smoker's—not a disturbing experience that calls for a cigarette to excite the brain and body once again.

So the sensuality of pipe smoking is akin to the sensuality that leads to sexual satisfaction and enjoyment. There are, no doubt, any number of pipe smokers who are not sexy at all and who perhaps love their pipes more than their women. But the evidence tells us that the average pipe smoker is adept at lighting up more than just his pipe.

9

THE MEDITATIVE MIND IS
A HEALTHY MIND

Daughter of Bacchus

Now the kind nymph of Bacchus borne
By Morpheus' daughter, she that seems
Gifted upon her natal morn
By him with fire, by her with dreams,
Nicotia, dearer to the Muse
Than all the grapes' bewildering juice.
We worship, unforbid of thee;
And, as her incense floats and curls
In airy spires and wayward whirls,
Or poises on its tremulous stalk
A flower of frailest revery,
So winds and loiters, idly free,
The current of unguided talk,
Now laughter-rippled, and now caught
In smooth, dark pools of deeper thought.

Meanwhile thou mellowest every word,
A sweetly unobtrusive third;
For thou hast magic beyond wine,
To unlock natures each to each;
The unspoken thought thou canst divine;
Thou fillest the pauses of the speech
With whispers that to dream-land reach,
And frozen fancy-springs unchain
In Arctic outskirts of the brain;
Sun of all inmost confidences!
To thy rays doth the heart unclose
Its formal calyx of pretences,
That close against rude day's offences,
And open its shy midnight rose . . .

—James Russell Lowell,
Under the Willows, *1869*

*T*he Indians of America not only invented the tobacco pipe, they revered it. The stately calumet with its bowl of red soapstone and the long stem of burnished ash was a sacred object. The calumet did not merely symbolize peace; it brought peace to its users, and the mythology connected with the pipe and the pungent herb smoked in it made it clear that pipe smoking was of divine origin.

For the Indians, as for millions of later pipe lovers, pipe smoking was a way to alter their state of consciousness. As the aromatic fumes were gently puffed, the world softly altered itself, reality lost its sharp and anxious edges, and the smoker was enveloped in a realm of inward repose.

Just as alcohol was a way of deliberately altering consciousness, so was the pipe (the "dry drink," as it was once called) a mind-altering device. But unlike alcohol, which could lead to violence as well as stupor, pipe smoking led only to contemplation and tranquillity. Like the prayer wheels of Tibetan lamas or the mandalas of the Hindus and Buddhists, the pipe evoked the presence of the deities and absorption in the divine.

Humans have always recognized that the merging of personal identity with the deity was a precious and soul-restoring experience. The yogis call this state *dhyana*, and reach it through disciplined practice; Japanese monks achieve it through *zazen* (Zen meditation); and Europeans and Americans are seeing ways of achieving this state through meditation, a positive and utterly healthful way of balancing and improving one's life.

Dr. Herbert Benson stripped meditation of its clinging religious overtones, encased it in Western medical terms, and wrote a best-selling book entitled *The Relaxation Response*. Dr. Benson suggests that the relaxation response can be triggered by four basic factors: (1) a quiet environment; (2) a mental device, such as a constant stimulus to shift the mind away from logical, externally oriented thought; (3) a passive attitude of nonattachment; and (4) a comfortable, relaxed posture.[12]

A pipe, like a mantra, is a device to "shift the mind away from logical, externally oriented thought." Pipe smoking, as secular as it may seem, is one of the most accepted and revered ways for Westerners to relax into a state of meditation. Centuries of Western literature have extolled this virtue.

In meditation there occurs a diminution of the field of awareness. The consciousness, normally focused on solving the problems of the external world, begins to refocus on a more limited and circumscribed field. Excessive stimulation is removed from awareness and the mind begins to concentrate its attention in one direction, undistracted. This quieting of the ever-distracted, ever-jumpy "monkey of the mind" is an alteration of consciousness that brings in its wake a peace.

It is Dr. Benson's understanding — as it has been that of thousands of meditators over thousands of years — that this respite from our normal, agitated state of consciousness is life-giving: it heals the body as well as the spirit. This is why he recommends it as a therapeutic tool.

In our earlier discussion of relaxation and physiological arousal, it was noted that the ability to relax is also the ability to trigger a parasympathetic state in our nervous system — a state of recuperation, restoration, and tissue rebuilding. One of the signs of relaxation in the central nervous system is a lowering of the frequency of brain waves. When our eyes and brains are open to the varied stimuli of the outer world, the electrical activity of the brain usually races along at a high frequency: from thirteen to twenty-five cycles per second or even higher. These busy and agitated frequencies are called beta waves, and are typical of a wide-awake state of mind. Beta waves normally reflect a dominance of the sympathetic nervous system.

When the nervous state changes to parasympathetic dominance, however, the frequency of brain waves can be expected to turn lower (certainly not in all sections of the brain, nor all the time, but the general tendency is a greater presence of lower frequencies). When brain waves slow to approximately twelve to eight cycles per second, they are referred to as alpha waves. The alpha frequency is associated with greater calmness and clarity of mind. There is less distraction and agitation, less emotional drive, and less "attachment" to external stimuli. The troubled waters of the mind become more placid and translucent.

There has been much excitement over the significance of alpha waves, particularly the way in which we can learn to elicit them through biofeedback training. Also there has been much nonsense and misunderstanding of the nature of alpha waves and their relation to states of consciousness. But Barbara Brown, one of the most respected authorities in this field, reminds us that despite some confusion in this area, "there are some forty or more research reports which indicate a role of alpha activity in states of emotion or consciousness characterized as a relatively tranquil, non-anxious, or inwardly directed. Moreover, *all* clinical reports to date, including extended studies, note remarkable shifts in behavior, emotions, and attitudes following alpha biofeedback. . . ."[13]

There is every evidence that the meditative mind is a healthy mind. And the Criswell Survey gives us every social evidence that the calm, leisurely demeanor of the pipe smoker is the sign of a meditative mind. Similarly, Eysenck's description of the "stable introvert" seems to indicate the pipe smoker's tendency toward meditation.

In another study, done in 1974, Criswell made a direct comparison of the brain waves of pipe smokers and cigarette smokers before, during, and after smoking. The results, although far from complete or conclusive, were highly interesting. With a group consisting of four cigarette smokers, four pipe smokers, and a control group of four nonsmokers, brain waves were sampled for five minutes before each subject smoked, ten minutes while he smoked, and five minutes after he smoked. The cigarette smokers showed a beginning baseline of only 32.19 percent alpha waves during the first five minutes, then a drop down to 28.11 percent alpha during the ten minutes of cigarette smoking, followed by a rebound of alpha up to 41 percent of the time during the five minutes after the cigarette was finished.

This downward plunge and upward surge of brain wave frequency suggests that the cigarette smoker is on a kind of neural roller coaster of considerable instability. By contrast, the pipe smokers established an initial baseline of 46.29 percent alpha—a surprising 14 percent more alpha than the cigarette smokers. During the ten-minute period of pipe smoking the four subjects actually *increased* the amount of alpha time to 48.58 percent, and during the five minutes following the smoking period the alpha time further increased to 49 percent.

Despite the limitations of the Criswell research, the evidence suggests two possibilities about pipe smokers: first, that pipe smokers tend to have a relatively high level of alpha wave activity (non-smokers began at 51.17 percent, dropped to 42.27 percent, then slid back up to 48.34 percent at the end of the experiment); and second, that pipe smokers have an extraordinarily steady brain wave state through the phases of smoking a pipe. The roller coaster ride of the cigarette smoker is, it seems, foreign to pipe smokers, who from the neurological point of view appear indeed to be "steady," "reliable," and "dependable" as well as "calm," "meditative," and "leisurely."

So, from yet another point of view, the pipe smoker shows himself again to be an amazingly stable and steady person. And we cannot help but speculate that, for him, the pipe is a way of maintaining and training himself in steadiness of composure—a composure that is meditative and contemplative in nature.

We have observed how hypnotic is the entire ritual of pipe smoking. Whether we say that he is invoking a meditative state or a relaxation response is immaterial; physiologically, it is the same state. Following Dr. Benson's four requirements, the pipe smoker usually (1) chooses a quiet place and time for his smoking; (2) chooses pipe and tobacco as the constant stimulus that shifts his mind away from the logical, externally oriented realm into a focus on the constant rhythm of puffing; (3) enjoys pipe smoking as an end in itself; and (4) assumes a comfortable posture when smoking.

There is one other thing about the relaxation response: it does not occur abruptly. It takes about fifteen or twenty minutes to trigger relaxation and the dominance of the parasympathetic system—about the time it takes to smoke a pipe. Unlike the cigarette, which provides a brief and arousing experience, the pipe takes time. It cannot be hurried. The slow and steady movements bring slowness and steadiness to the mind, leading the pipe smoker to a meditative state wherein he, the pipe, and the pulselike rhythm of puffing fuse and become as one.

PART III

A
SENSUAL GUIDE
TO THE ART OF
PIPE SMOKING

10

THE ODOR AND TASTE
OF TOBACCO

*Being at sea, about midway between Santa Maria and the large island which
I named Fernandina, we met a man in a canoe going from Santa Maria to
Fernandina. He had with him a piece of bread which the natives make as big
as one's fist . . . and some dried leaves which are highly valued among them,
for a quantity thereof was brought me (as a gift) at San Salvador. . . .*

— *Christopher Columbus, ship's log, October 25, 1492*

The word "tobacco" has a tangled history. Originally *tobaco* or *tobago* was a Carib Indian word that referred not to the tobacco leaf, but to the device in which the leaf was smoked — a corn shuck or some other heavy wrapping in which the leaf was contained for the purpose of smoking. Apparently, when Europeans brought tobacco back home, they mistakenly called the herb by the name of the wrapper. Right or wrong, it's been tobacco ever since. Today tobacco is grown in some eighty different countries; yet the origin of every single plant can be traced to the same source, the American Indians, and the United States remains the greatest exporter of tobacco in the world.

The variety of tobaccos grown around the world and here in the United States is staggering. A single type of domestic tobacco may have as many as 170 different grades. This means that the choice of taste, aroma, cut, flavor, and burning qualities can be combined into virtually an unlimited number of blends.

Cigarette smokers remain largely unaware of this immense variety, because the range of cigarette blends is quite limited. The situation has not been improved with the introduction of the filter cigarette, which demands only tobaccos with a taste that is strong enough to survive the filtration process. Pipe smokers, however, have a wondrous choice of tobacco flavors available, both in commercial blends and in custom blends they can have made at a tobacconist.

The choice of tobacco is just as personal and individual as the choice of a pipe, and the pipe smoker should be aware of his options. The knowledgeable pipe smoker will be familiar with the leaf, grade, cut, and curing process of his favorite tobaccos.

In general, tobaccos are either air-cured, flue-cured or smoke-cured. Burley, the basic component of all American-style pipe tobaccos, is normally air-cured. After harvesting, 90 percent of all burley is strung on poles and hung in barns to dry under natural conditions for four to six weeks.

Burley's neutral, mellow taste and aroma makes it an ideal tobacco for blending with other tobaccos or flavorings. The majority of American mixtures begin with burley, and it comprises about one-third of all the tobacco grown in the United States.

Flue-cured tobaccos, such as the golden Virginia types, are hung in artificially heated barns and dried during a four- to six-day period under carefully controlled temperature and humidity conditions.

Virginia tobacco is grown not only in that state, but also in North and South Carolina, Kentucky, Georgia, Alabama, and Florida. Its big, yellow to dark brown leaf has fewer oils than burley but much more sugar, which gives it a mild, sweet taste.

Smoke-cured tobacco has a smoky, "plum pudding" taste, which is acquired by being smoked over smoldering fires of pine, myrtle, and other fragrant woods. Although some American tobaccos are cured in this manner, it is the latakia tobaccos of Syria and Cyprus that are famed for this aromatic quality, which makes them a favorite blend with the milder American tobaccos.

Maryland tobacco is cultivated only the state of Maryland. It has thin leaves that are quite neutral in both taste and aroma. Like burley, it blends well with other tobaccos and flavorings. It also has the most ideal burning qualities — not too hot, not too slow. If your tobacco burns too slowly or the blend is too heavy, the addition of a small amount of Maryland will improve it on either count.

Another domestic tobacco is perique, grown only in one circum-scribed area in Louisiana near New Orleans. Perique is a remarkable tobacco, cured by a process invented by the Choctaw and Chicasaw Indians. After a brief air-drying period, the leaves are packed in casks under great pressure and allowed to ferment in their own juices. The end result is a heady flavor utterly without bite, which adds both aroma and a spicy accent to all mixes. Never smoked by itself, perique is used as a blend in very small quantities — about 3 percent would be quite sufficient in a blend of 72 percent burley and 25 percent Virginia.

Cavendish is a tobacco that has steadily grown in popularity be-cause of its sweet taste. Lord William Cavendish, Duke of Newcastle, developed a variety of tobacco in 1660 that bore his name; but there is no leaf grown today that is called cavendish. Instead, cavendish now refers to two different things: (1) a flavoring process designed to sweeten the taste, and (2) a particular cut of tobacco, somewhere between a ribbon cut and a heavy fine cut.

The cavendish tobaccos manufactured in Holland, Denmark, and the United States are heavily impregnated with casing sauces and flavorings to ensure a sweet taste. In Great Britain, where tobacco manufacturing laws have long forbade use of casing sauces, the cavendish flavor is achieved in this way: heavier grades of

Virginia flue-cured tobacco are packed into molds for several days, and the pressure causes the natural oils to rise. Because Virginia leaf has a heavy natural sugar content, the resulting product is quite sweet. In another version, the tobacco is steamed and we get a black cavendish.

Latakia is an oriental (not Turkish) type of tobacco that is aromatic, slow burning, and has its own "plum pudding" taste, which is a result of being smoke-cured over a mixture of fragrant woods and leaves. Latakia originally came only from the Syrian town of Latakia on the Mediterranean coast; most of the latakia used today, however, comes from Cyprus. As is the case with cavendish, the name does not describe the tobacco leaf but the curing process.

Because of its strength, latakia is never blended with fruit-flavored aromatic tobaccos. Like perique, it is to be used sparingly — from 1 to 5 percent, blended with milder tobaccos. A mixture of 72 percent burley, 25 percent Virginia, and 3 percent latakia would be a suitable blend. Depending on how much the smoker likes plum pudding, the amount of latakia could be increased to 10 percent or more.

The topic of oriental tobaccos is a matter of some confusion, primarily because these are frequently referred to as Turkish. Turkey, however, is only one producer of these highly prized tobaccos; they also come from Greece, Yugoslavia, Bulgaria, and Russia. In general, oriental tobaccos are characterized by being aromatic or semi-aromatic, of low nicotine content (thus mild in flavor), and cut from a leaf that is much smaller than the large American burley and Virginia leaves which may grow as large as one foot in width and two feet in length.

Oriental tobaccos grown strictly in Turkey are the Smyrna (Izmir), Samsun-Maden, Baffra, and Trebizond. Smyrna is one of the most widely used Turkish tobaccos, constituting almost 70 percent of Turkish tobacco production. It is very sweet, lightly aromatic, and blends easily with almost any kind of tobacco. Samsun, used in high-quality tobacco blends, is grown only in the Black Sea region. The Turks consider it one of the finest tobaccos in the world. Baffra is similar to Samsun but with darker leaves and a pungent odor. Trebizond, with its strong taste and aroma, is usually not exported but is a favorite within Turkey.

Although some highly esteemed oriental tobaccos are produced in Bulgaria, Russia, and Yugoslavia, very little of it ever reaches Western pipes. But this is more than made up for by the Greek tobaccos, especially the famous Basma, referred to by the Greeks as "the king of tobaccos." With its small leaves and fine, velvety vein system, Basma tobacco has gained favor for its unusually sweet and refreshing taste and its good burning qualities. Other Greek tobaccos that are somewhat similar are known as Xanthi, Djebel, Mahalla, Dubek, Kavalla, and Yeniji.

So informed about the varieties of pipe tobacco, the pipe smoker can begin to discover or create the blend that suits his individual taste. But there are still more factors to be considered, among them the very important matter of what the manufacturer *then* does with the cured leaf. Milt Sherman, one of the most knowledgeable of American tobacco men, has pointed out that the manufacturer's concern is to be sure that the final blend consists of well-mixed grains that have both a uniformity of taste and a burning rate that is neither too fast (hot) nor too slow (hard to burn).[14]

Whatever the blend, says Sherman, its burning qualities will be determined by four factors: (1) the type of tobacco, (2) the moisture content, (3) the type of cut, and (4) the amount of flavoring. We have already discussed how complex the choice of tobacco can be. The degree of moisture is controlled at various stages of manufacture by deliberate drying of the leaf, followed by an exact period of steaming to ensure that the tobacco has a uniform moisture content. As a secondary precaution, all large manufacturers have total control of the humidity within the production area.

The pipe smoker has a choice of many variations on four basic cuts of tobacco. Granulated tobacco is cut into irregularly shaped flakes of medium size (1/16 inch or less), so that when it is packed into the pipe, air spaces between the flakes will allow the tobacco to burn slowly and coolly. Cube-cut tobacco is a shade larger, and as its name suggests each flake is in the shape of a cube. It burns much as granulated tobacco does. Shag- or long-cut tobacco has thin, long strands from ½- to 1-inch in length, which allow more circulation of air and faster burning. Plug-cut tobacco is sold as a solid cake, which the smoker then crumbles into loose tobacco. Its density slows down the rate of burning.

There are many other types of cuts that vary from these four basic forms. Pipe smokers will find some domestic as well as foreign pipe tobaccos designated as rough cut, crimp cut, fine cut, ribbon cut, cavendish cut, crushed plug, slice cut, ready rubbed, and flake cut. A point to remember is that longer, larger cuts indicate that the blend is made only from destemmed leaf tobacco, and is thus of high quality.

The flavoring of the tobacco can make a big difference in the desired taste and aroma of the blend. Three separate procedures may be used in the flavoring process: concentrated flavorings, casing sauces, and top dressings.

Some of the flavorings added to tobacco are chocolate, vanilla, menthol, rum, licorice, a variety of fruit flavors, and several wine flavors such as burgundy, sherry, and Madeira. These flavorings are fixed into the tobacco by the casing sauce, which consists of a resin-type chemical, water, water-soluble sugars, and humectants such as sorbitol, propylene or glycerine. Thus the casing sauce serves not only to fix the flavor but also to control the moisture content. Neutral tobaccos such as burley and Maryland accept casing sauces easily, as much again as their own weight. Virginia tobacco, however, accepts very little. Sometimes top dressings of tonka bean, cocoa bean, or deertongue leaves are added to the blend. Top dressings give the tobacco a special aroma.

The cultivation, curing, and manufacture of tobacco is a richly

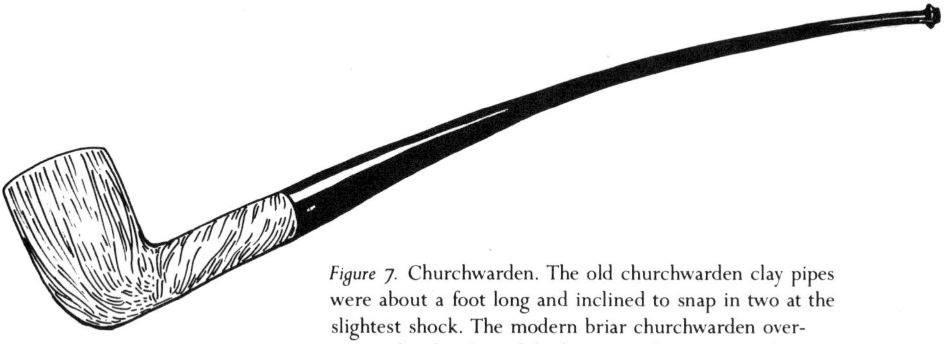

Figure 7. Churchwarden. The old churchwarden clay pipes were about a foot long and inclined to snap in two at the slightest shock. The modern briar churchwarden overcomes this fragility of the long stem by using a vulcanite stem. The churchwarden shape has functional advantages different from the pot shape: its long stem allows the air to become optimally cool before being puffed. The churchwarden is easy to hold when seated and it is unexcelled for aroma, i.e., the bowl's distance from the face allows the smoke an optimum thinning and dilution before reaching the nostrils.

complex process, steeped in tradition and romance. Nowhere is this better displayed than in that transitional moment when mounds of harvested and cured tobacco sit in long rows waiting to be auctioned to the tobacco manufacturers. The huge auction barns are turned dark gold by the burnished light emanating from the tobacco piles, and the air has a honeyed density that crowds into the nostrils. The farmers stand over to one side, watching a long cortege of men who slowly make their way along gilded rows. The auctioneer's mysterious gabble quietly fills the barn with its imperturbable rhythm, the buyers nod and gesture their bids, and the auction house accountant notes the buyer and the price of each sale. It is a colorful and ever-impressive ritual that reaches its denouement only when a pipe smoker, at some later and magical moment, unseals the can, lifts off the lid and breathes in a heady aroma that sets him dreaming.

THE LOOK AND FEEL
OF THE PIPE

Tube, I love thee as my life;
By thee I mean to choose a wife.
Tube, thy colour *let me find*
In her skin, *and in her* mind.
Let her have a shape *as fine;*
Let her breath be sweet as thine;
Let her, when her lips I kiss,
Burn *like thee, to give me bliss;*
Let her in some smoke or other,
All my failings kindly smother.
Often when my thoughts are low,

Send them where they ought *to go.*
When to study I incline,
Let her aid be such as thine:
Such as thine the charming pow'r,
In the vacant social hour.
Let her live to give delight,
Ever warm and ever bright:
Let her deeds, whene'er she dies,
Mount as incense to the skies.

— *Anonymous, eighteenth century*

A pipe is basically any sort of long, narrow tube through which air can pass. When a reed is blown through, it makes a certain sound, and our word "pipe" is derived from a Latin word meaning "peep," to describe this sound. When one sucks on the reed, drawing in the fumes of burning tobacco or some other herb, it becomes a smoking pipe.

Although the American Indians were not the only people to invent the smoking pipe, they appear to have been the first; pipes have been found in their burial mounds that date back six thousand years. Archaeological diggings have also disclosed that pipes were

77

used in Europe long before the appearance of tobacco. Iron and terra-cotta pipes have been found throughout the British Isles, and on the continent from France to Russia.

The basic structure of most pipes is twofold, consisting of the container (in English it is called the bowl, in French it is a *fourneau* "furnace") into which the tobacco is put and the tube, or the stem, through which it is smoked. This simple structure has been elaborated on over the years, and the pipe looks like this in section:

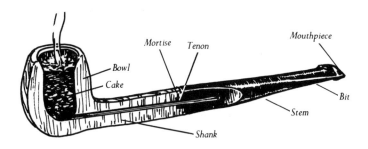

Figure 8. A simple modern briar, cutaway.

The contemporary tobacco pipe is the product of centuries of craftsmanship. Each part has its own special significance, and the knowledgeable pipe buyer should observe with great care before buying. What follows is a general discussion of what to look for in a pipe. Since most smokers — especially beginning pipe smokers — will be purchasing a briar, we will focus first on this type of pipe.

One of the most important rules is not to buy a cheap pipe. Cheap briar pipes are predictably bad pipes which will burn hot, smell evil, and ruin the taste of the tobacco. In fact, no matter how good the tobacco, an equally good pipe is essential to its proper enjoyment. Be prepared to pay a goodly price if you intend to have a goodly smoke. But even a costly pipe can be defective. To avoid disappointment, study the following components of the pipe carefully.

The Bowl

It is crucial that the bowl of the pipe not smoke too hot. Not only will a hot bowl burn the fingers, it will turn the tobacco in the chamber into a bubbling mass on the bottom as well as the top, fouling the aroma, overheating the smoke, and clogging the air hole. Because a pipe bowl is essentially a furnace its wall must provide proper insulation. In general, thick-walled pipes will feel cooler and smoke cooler than thin-walled pipes. The classic billiard pipe, with walls as thin as 3/16 inch, is perhaps a minimum. If the briar is excellent, such a pipe will smoke well for years. Small pipes or pipes with thin walls are to be avoided; they may be cute and they may be light, but they will surely be thrown away in due time.

In addition to a sufficient thickness, the bowl must not be too shallow. To ensure the perfect puff, the tobacco must be in a vertical column that is taller than it is thick. Why? A pipe that is too squat will not nurture the fire — it will not burn all the tobacco, but only that in the middle. In addition, the best taste comes from a slow vertical descent of the burn, where the tobacco at the bottom serves as a cool filter for the smoke that comes from the burning upper layers. This bottom tobacco becomes the dottle; it is the last part to be smoked, and for many smokers it is the best part, because of its richness.

Having examined the bowl for thickness and depth, you should check its shape and texture. Be sure that the top of the chamber is wider than the bottom; otherwise it will burn unevenly and hot. As to texture, check on two things. If there is varnish on the inside, you are looking at an inferior pipe that is dressing up the appearance of poor briar. Moreover, the varnish will volatilize, forming an unpleasant chemical cake on the chamber walls. Examine the interior texture for pits or imperfections. If you see any, it means that the pipe will probably suffer an early death by burning out through those very spots.

It is not a serious matter if there are surface imperfections on the outside of the bowl; in fact, this may be an important piece of good fortune for the beginning smoker who needs a good briar at a reasonable cost. Briar is a precious and expensive wood, and perfect-grain briar pipes are rare. Most of the pipe bowls made out of each briar block will have minor imperfections, often caused by pebbles that have been encased in the briar during its long growth (up to 250 years). Imperfect briar bowls with small pits on the outside are called "seconds." Filler is added to the pits to smooth out the bowl, and such pipes are sold at a lower price. They are often excellent buys.

Even though English and American pipe smokers prefer straight-grained pipes, this has little to do with the quality of the briar. The grain can be transverse or filled with bird's-eyes, and still be just as fine a smoke. What is important is the *closeness* of the grain. This indicates that the bowl has been turned from the densest part of the briar block and not from its trunk.

Close-grained briar pipes are objects of considerable beauty. The whorls, streamings, fibers, and arabesques are a delight to the eye and a promise to the nose and palate. The bowl of a fine briar, colored by months of careful smoking, has an irresistible allure. Veteran smokers can often be seen rubbing the warm bowl against the sides of their noses so that the skin oils will bring out the intricate scrollwork of the briar wall.

The Stem and Mouthpiece

Pipe stems can be made of a variety of substances from simple cane to precious amber, but the finest material is a light, tasteless rubber material called vulcanite or ebonite. Many European pipes have stems of horn, the grain of which is lovely. But mouthpieces of horn are a bit thick (and in the case of the Alsatian, round) and this is uncomfortable for some smokers. Horn eventually wears down and collapses. Wood stems, of course, also collapse after a short, wet period of time.

Amber stems are traditionally associated with meerschaum pipes, to which they add a final luxury. Amber is fossilized resin of pine, formed thousands of years ago during the Tertiary period. The color varies from pale yellow to hyacinth red. Genuine amber stems (remember — there are plastic imitations) are, when found, quite expensive. On the other hand, they are also inflammable, a fact which may comfort you if you do not possess such a stem.

Vulcanite is hard without being brittle, long lasting, and can be shaped in many convenient forms. The only thing to watch out for is whether the vulcanite is varnished or has mold lines on the side; in either case, it is cheap and worthless. Vulcanite stems can be thick or thin. "Fish-tail" mouthpieces are flattened out and widened, distributing the pressure of the smoker's mouth over a wide area of the bite. For most smokers, this is the most comfortable and least fatiguing mouthpiece. Novelty pipes that lack a mouthpiece are a nuisance; the pipe constantly slides out of the mouth unless it is held by hand. And be sure there is a lip at the end of the stem.

Another matter is the size of the hole at the end of the bit. A small, round one concentrates the heat and smoke in one spot in the mouth, whereas a wide orifice allows a cooler dispersion of the smoke, thus a cooler tongue. This is no small matter.

The shape and length of the stem are a different matter. Whether it is thick or thin, round, square, or diagonal, the shape should gracefully complement the bowl of the pipe so that it will appear light and well balanced to the hand as well as the eye.

Whether the stem is curved or straight makes a difference to many smokers. With a straight stem, the smoke goes straight up from the faraway bowl, thus robbing the nose of the aroma. A curved stem serves the nose better. The French pipe fancier, Georges Herment, has observed that it is universal among pipe smokers to notice that the aroma of another's pipe is always more appealing than one's own.[15] Because the aroma is inseparable from the taste of the tobacco, long stems such as the churchwarden, or big curved stems like the Oom-Paul and the calabash can provide exquisite moments of pipe smoking. Another point to keep in mind is that long stems, like thick bowls, cool the smoke.

Filters

Many American-made pipes come equipped with a metal filter, which is a perfectly useless device. Very fine pipes will normally not contain such a contraption, but occasionally they are put in the pipe to attract buyers who have decided to quit cigarettes and try a pipe to cut down on tar and nicotine. Filters, whether metal or fiber, are set in pipes in order to make money — not to make a better smoke. The beginning smoker would be well advised to remove the filter before smoking his pipe; it clogs the air channel, diminishes the flavor, and befouls the pipe with its accumulation of tars. If the filter is permanently built into the stem, don't buy the pipe.

These are the primary matters to be considered when examining a pipe for purchase. One could, of course, assume that a very expensive pipe will not have any of the flaws that we have mentioned as possibilities. But price guarantees nothing. A fifty-dollar pipe can be a fifty-dollar disaster, for not all pipe makers are reputable. Some of those that are consistently dependable are both worldwide in fame and sky-high in price: Dunhill, Comoy, and Charatan in England; Sixteen Ivarsson, Stanwell, and Nording in Denmark; Savanelli in Italy; Peterson in Ireland.

But pipes of similarly high quality can be found in France. After all, the French invented the briar pipe. The cunning pipe buyer who keeps his eyes open to the various factors we have mentioned could do no better than to visit the famous French pipe-making towns of Gogolin, in the Department of Var, or Saint-Claude in the Jura section of eastern France. There he could find the pipe of his dreams. Saint-Claude, the birthplace of the briar pipe, is said to produce the most carefully fashioned, best-finished, and most luxurious pipes in the world.

12

THE CAKING, FILLING AND LIGHTING OF THE PIPE

My Pipe

My pipe is old/ And caked with soot;
My wife remarks:/ "How can you put
That horrid relic,/ So unclean,
Inside your mouth?/ The nicotine
Is strong enough/ To stupefy
A Swedish plumber."/ I reply:

"This is the kind/ Of pipe I like:
I fill it full/ Of Happy Strike,
Or Barking Cat/ Or Cabman's Puff
Or Brooklyn Bridge/ (That potent stuff)
Or Chaste Embraces,/ Knacker's Twist
Old Honeycomb/ Or Niggerfist

I clamp my teeth/ Upon its stem —
It is my bliss,/ My diadem.
Whate'er fate/ May do to me,
This is my favorite
        B

  B   B

For this dear pipe/ You feign to scorn
I smoked the night/ The boy was born."

— *Christopher Morley,* Poems

Caking the Pipe

A fine brandy achieves its fullest flavor and bouquet only when it is placed within specially charred wooden casks. It is the same with a fine tobacco: the taste and aroma are at their peak only when the burning tobacco is encased within a bowl that is properly charred around its inner surface. This lining of char — the "cake" of the pipe — is indispensable for the full enjoyment of pipe smoking.

Once a pipe smoker has the tobacco he wants and the pipe he wants, he will set out to build up a cake around the bowl's interior walls — and he will build it as slowly and carefully as a stone mason, from the bottom up. This wall of char insulates the pipe wood from the bowl's heat and controls the temperature so as to produce the maximum taste and aroma.

Pipe smokers are ever mindful that what they are holding in their hands is little more than a furnace with a stem stuck into it, and this portable furnace becomes intensely hot. At 250 degrees centigrade, nicotine vaporizes and much of the substance of the tobacco is transmuted into carbon. The carbon adheres to the walls of the pipe, forming a layer of insulation that (when evenly caked) creates an even distribution of heat within the bowl.

The bowl of any pipe, be it briar, meerschaum, porcelain, clay, or corncob, will begin charring as of the first smoke. This occurs automatically and cannot be prevented by the smoker (nor should it be). But he can prevent an uneven distribution of the cake by following a few simple rules.

First of all, the smoker should inspect the new bowl to see if any varnish or finish is on the inner wall. The inner wall must be free of any substance, so that only the wood itself will bind with the char; volatilized chemical substances will give the cake an unpleasant flavor. If there is anything on the inner walls, it should be rubbed out or even lightly sanded away with fine-grain sandpaper. A gentle and traditional way of scouring the bowl is to set the pipe in an ashtray, stem slightly up, and then fill the bowl with brandy, rum, or some other alcohol mix for a few days. The action of the alcohol is exactly like a slow flame, scouring and opening up the inner wooden walls, leaving the wood clean and ready for the first pipeful.

Once the bowl is clean, the smoker is ready for his first smoke and his first venture in building up a perfect cake. The first five or six times the pipe is smoked the bowl should be filled only one-quarter full. In this way the cake will gradually form from the bottom up. The smoker who, from the beginning, fills his pipe to the brim, will find cake forming at the top of the bowl, crowding the air passage. By building carefully from the bottom up, a smooth and even char will form. The pipe smoker can aid this early caking process by

Figure 9. Bulldog With Saddle Bit. This shape is particularly popular in France and Great Britain. The bulldog is like a large pear. It has lots of wood and, when properly caked, can have a bowl whose walls are almost ½-inch thick. Note that the saddle bit is not only abruptly tapered into a flat bit but that the shank and stem are square rather than round. This squareness gives a very special feeling when the pipe is gripped. This is a macho pipe.

wetting the bottom quarter of the bowl with a bit of water or honey just before putting in the tobacco.

After the first half-dozen smokes, the tobacco should be increased to the half-bowl level for another five or six times, then just barely filled to the top for six more smokes. Within two dozen pipefuls, your pipe should be well seasoned and well caked, ready to give you "the perfect puff."

Filling the Pipe

Once the cake of carbon has formed around the inner walls of the bowl, the pipe can be filled to the brim and smoked. It is not, however, a matter of sticking the pipe in a can of tobacco and ramming the bowl full of tobacco leaf. Stuffing the bowl any old way with a wad of tobacco can result in one of two misfortunes: either the pipe will be packed too loosely and will smoke hot and fast; or the pipe will be packed too tightly to draw well, and will have to be emptied and repacked. So, rather than risk either of these two extremes, the patient and pleasure-seeking pipe smoker will fill his pipe in stages.

The veteran proceeds somewhat as follows. First he picks up the pipe and blows through the stem to be sure it is clear. Next he checks the bowl to be sure that the dottle at the bottom of the bowl has been knocked out and that no loose flakes of tobacco are left that might clog the stem. After this initial inspection, the first pinch of tobacco is put into the bottom of the bowl. The first pinch is the smallest pinch of tobacco, and it is carefully and softly laid down over the hole so as not to clog it. The finger is used as a final check on the evenness of this first pinch.

Another pinch is added and pressed down, and so on until the bowl is filled. The final pinch of tobacco at the brim of the pipe should be carefully pressed down and evened all over its surface. If the pipe has been packed with just the right degree of density, the air will draw softly through the bowl. The secret to obtaining just the right density is very simple: *as each pinch is added, press it down more firmly than the previous one.* In filling his pipe, the smoker is always seeking the golden mean—not too much, not too little. This is quickly learned after a few trials.

Obviously, the way in which a pipe is packed is quite different from the way tobacco is packed into a cigarette. The tobacco in a cigarette is uniform in its density, which is why a machine can be used to make many thousands per hour. But pipe tobacco can ony be properly layered into a pipe, denser layers on top of lighter layers, by the subtle differentiations in pressure from the finger. Experienced pipe smokers have highly intelligent fingers, which can create a pipeful, every time, in which the stack of tobacco has the proper density throughout.

Here are a few other tips about filling the bowl. Coarser cut tobacco is superior to fine-cut for packing, because it is less likely to clog the bowl. Many smokers will shake the pouch, bringing up the coarser flakes, and use it for the bottom pinches. Another thing to remember is that drier tobacco packs in a springier manner than moist tobacco, and it will draw better. If the tobacco is old and dry, it could pack so loosely that the pipe smokes hot. The remedy for this is to mix in fresh tobacco with the old to obtain a more balanced moisture content. By the same token, tobacco that is moist will often clog up the bowl, forcing the smoker to empty the pipe and start all over again. There are many tricks that pipe smokers use to maintain the moisture level in their stored tobacco — from bits of damp blotting paper or slices of apple in the jar to special gadgets sold in the tobacco shops. We will leave you to discover your own best system.

The proper filling and caking of the pipe guarantees not only the sweetness of the smoke but the longevity of the pipe. Whether the bowl is made of porcelain, meerschaum, or wood, the insulating layer of carbon within it gives maximum protection from cracking or burnout during smoking as well as the fragile period of cooling the pipe.

Lighting the Pipe

So, you have the pipe, you have the tobacco, and you have the tobacco properly layered and pressed into the bowl. All that remains is to light up. Two questions naturally arise: "With what?" and "How?" These seemingly simple questions have rather involved answers.

What you light the pipe *with* is a matter of some importance. For example, if you strike a sulfur match or a waxed match and light your pipe immediately, the sulfur or wax odors from the ignition will quickly adhere to the tobacco, ruining the taste. Let the foul chemicals burn away before you use the match. Some substances make better lights than others. In Europe, the traditional means of lighting a pipe was to steal a small ember from the fireplace. Even now veteran pipe smokers testify that the finest light and the finest puffing comes from placing an ember into the center of the bowl and allowing it to burn its way downward during the course of the smoke.

But inasmuch as roaring hearths and ardent embers are not always available, other means can be used. One is the mechanical pipe lighter with flintstone, steel wheel, wick, lighter fluid, and flame guard, though it may be difficult to find an odorless lighter fuel. Such lighters have a generous flame and can be used outdoors as well as in. Paper book matches are to be avoided as too short and chemically treated, but ordinary wooden kitchen matches are excellent.

So with match in hand or ember in pincers, the pipe smoker proceeds to light the pipe in the proper manner. *Light the bowl evenly, from the middle out to the perimeter.* The flame of the match descends into the center of the bowl, the smoker puffs lightly, the surface tobacco crisps, turns ashen, and yields itself upward in a flash of flame and blue smoke, then the flame is applied in a slow spiral outward, until the entire surface is smoking. At this point, the fire usually goes out, abruptly,

It takes two matches to start a pipe. The first match produces a burn-off of the top surface of the tobacco, and the second match launches the full and continuous smoke. Between the first and second match, the just-burned surface tobacco must be smoothed down with the thumb or lightly tamped and evened with a pipe tool. By pressing down the ashes and smoothing the surface, it is possible to see how evenly the tobacco has burned and where the flame has not yet touched. This done, the second match is evenly applied to the whole of the surface and *if* the pipe is well filled and *if* the pipe is well puffed, it will burn without stopping, right down through the dottle at the bottom of the bowl, leaving naught but ashes and heady enjoyment.

The lighting of the pipe always takes place with the bowl in an upright position, so that the flame goes straight down and so that the pipe smoker can see what he is doing. Amateur pipe smokers can often be seen turning their pipes sideways when lighting up, believing that more flame enters the bowl. Unfortunately, the line of draft of a slanted pipe is usually crooked and uncentered, igniting the tobacco away from the center of the pipe. This creates uneven burning, uneven caking, and the danger of a burnout, not to mention a less than satisfactory taste. Even worse is the amateur's practice of turning the bowl upside down to light up. In this position it is impossible to see the exact position of the flame; but even worse, the smoker is unwittingly burning the top of the pipe bowl. A meerschaum that is lit upside down will be irrevocably scarred.

Perhaps the most important aspect of lighting and smoking a pipe is the puff itself, which should be easy, short, unrushed, unforced, and steady. After all is said and done, after the rules have been followed and each procedure carefully carried out, it is the puffer sitting behind the stem who determines how good the smoke is going to be. Caught between the Scylla of burning out and the Charybdis of going out, the cunning pipe smoker knows that his ultimate resource is his knowledge of how to puff — not too much, not too little, but just right.

13

THE EXQUISITE PLEASURE
OF PUFFING

Ashes to Dust

Sweet enchantment of my solitude,
Companion glowing-pipe-sublime delight;
To my dull'd soul thou bringst clear sight,
To my sad heart a calm and happy mood.
Tobacco rapture of my mind, when I
See, like the lightning, vanish in the air
Thy smoke, I find an image striking rare
Of my life's feebleness and brevity.
With eloquence thou tellst unto me
What I, alas! must one day be —
I, animated ashes — and I feel
Confused, ashamed, that, running after smoke,
I lose myself, like thee; thou dost evoke
Regrets when most thou dost thy charms reveal.

— Ascribed to Esprit de Raimond de
Mormoiron, Comte de Modene, and to
Johann G. Grave

*I*t is already dusk when he reaches the cabin. The air is misty, and the chill of night is already creeping about the shadows beneath the oak trees. The boots make a heavy sound as he steps onto the porch. Over to the side against the wall of the cabin is a low pile of wood — oak split into quarters and halves, the bright inner surface glowing dully in the fading light.

He cradles a pile of split logs in his arms, goes to the door, and turns the knob with his free hand. Inside, the only light comes from the embers in the fireplace, banked up and glowing since lunchtime. He sets the logs down by the fireplace, then turns on the lamp next to the reading chair. A soft yellowish light courses down onto the old overstuffed chair, the side table, the hassock, and the cowhide rug that lies by the hearth.

After he rakes up the embers he covers them with kindling wood and then adds the logs. The kindling cracks, sputters, and stretches itself into flame. The sounds and smells of the fire follow him as he goes into the kitchen. Coffee and water are put into the pot and set on the stove. Within minutes the pot hiccoughs a few times, then begins percolating. Because the cabin is still cold, he keeps on his mackinaw.

He opens the cupboard and takes out a bottle of brandy. Three fingers of amber liquid are poured into a tumbler, then a little water from the tap. As the odor of coffee begins to finger its way through the chilly air of the kitchen, he takes out a coffee mug and saucer. He sets them on the cabinet next to the tumbler and fills the mug. Then, carrying coffee and brandy, he returns to the livingroom and to the fire, which is now blazing lustily, drawing air into its maw and sending it roaring up the chimney.

Setting the glassware down on the side table, he takes the poker and rearranges the logs. This done, he takes off his boots, eases back into the overstuffed chair, sighs, and stretches his legs out on top of the hassock. For a long while he sits, transfixed by the dancing fire. Eventually, he lifts the brandy and takes a slow sip, still mesmerized by the flames. He chases the brandy with the coffee, not so much drinking it as holding the hot mug tilted against his face while he smells and sips the dark liquid.

The day is over and has been well spent. He has finished his afternoon chores, and now he sits quietly, alert but not fatigued, enjoying the sweet luxury of solitude. The early night cries of a hoot owl drift in from outdoors. He glances out the window and sees that it is black outside.

He finishes his brandy and coffee at the same time, taking the last drop from the glass and following it with the last remaining sip of coffee. He sets the glass and mug aside and begins looking over the little circular pipe rack within whose embrace stands a tobacco canister. There are six pipes in the rack: a heavy Oom-Paul, a slim bent briar, a classic billiard briar, a Canadian, an applewood, and a cherrywood pipe.

After unhurried deliberation he reaches over and picks up the long-shanked Canadian, puts the bit to his lips, and blows through it several times. Then he lightly taps the bowl on the round piece of cork in the middle of the ashtray. Holding the pipe up so that the lamplight reaches down to the bottom of the bowl, he sees a vagrant flake of tobacco at the bottom and removes it with the spoon of his pipe tool. This done, he brings the bowl up to his nose and sniffs it, savoring the faint sweetness of the cake which rises smoothly from the bottom of the bowl to the top.

He notices that the bit is turned slightly off center, and gently twists it until the flange is on the same level as the bottom of the bowl. For a while he lets his gaze fall over the pipe, enjoying its shape. Tiny and voluptuous in the hollow of his palm, the dark nut-colored grain flows from the bowl out into the long, smoke-cooling wooden shank.

This prolonged intimacy of touch and look and smell unfolds with languorous slowness. The more he gazes at the pipe, the more relaxed he becomes. It is as if this small piece of wood and vulcanite were the dwelling place of some animal spirit that had, amongst its powers, the ability to hypnotize. It is obvious that the fireplace, which until that time had occupied the center of his attention, was now becoming the glowing background and framework for a single, compelling object: the pipe.

The proper moment reached, he lifts up the tobacco canister and sets it in his lap. He removes the lid and lays it on the table, lodging the canister securely between his legs. Holding the pipe with his left hand, placing it over the mouth of the canister, he reaches with his right hand down into the tobacco store. The leaf is soft and slightly moist, and as his fingers lift the dark strands, the indescribably rich odor of burley wafts upward, mixing with the earthy aromas of the oak fire.

He takes a small amount of tobacco and inserts it into the pipe bowl. Using his little finger as a plunger, he deftly spreads this first pinch smoothly over the floor of the pipe. Before he puts in the next pinch, he lightly sucks through the stem to be sure that it is not clogged. With each small pinch he presses down then draws lightly on the stem. Within a minute the bowl is filled, and he shakes the excess into the canister, smoothing the top and evening the edges with his fingernail. The pipe is ready.

The next step delights him. Leaning over toward the fireplace, he rakes some of the coals toward the edge of the hearth. With the poker, he breaks up one of the coals into small pieces, then takes a pair of long tweezers from the table, picks up one small ember from the fireplace, and places it with great care into the exact center of the pipe bowl.

His eyes are fixed unwaveringly on the glowing coal as he brings the stem of the pipe to his mouth. His lips make a delicate puckering motion, sucking a tiny bit of air through the stem, which he then moves away from his lips a bit. He continues to gaze at the ember. With a small movement, he brings the stem to his lips again and, like a child attempting to suck the precious droplet of elixir from a honeysuckle flower, sips at the pipe. This time a little fumerole of gray-blue smoke erupts from the center of the bowl. As the fire spreads outward in a gray circle of ash, the ember slowly settles downward into the tobacco. The entire surface of the tobacco is now lit.

Like a subtle shifting of gears, his sipping changes from a light, intermittent pattern to a slower and easier rhythm. The smoker has settled into his smoke, every feeling, every movement, every glance centered on the small pipe of portable fire. The mouth makes a movement that is ever so gentle; the center of the tobacco seems to

Figure 10. Dublin With Saddle Bit. This is a graceful pipe which, with minor differences, may be called a Woodstock or a Yacht pipe.

drop as its surface smoke is drawn down to the stem, emerging from the mouth in a soft puff of smoke. The process is silent save for the occasional tiny explosion of an overly moist flake of tobacco. Clearly, an alchemical process is taking place; base matter is being artfully transmuted into something transcendent.

This magical relation between smoker and pipe is like a game, like a dance, and like making love. There is no hurry; the goal is already assured. It is merely a matter of enjoying each delicious moment in the process. The pipe is caressed, cuddled, and kissed; and it returns this adoration with warmth, richness, and satisfaction.

This ecstatic liaison of smoker and pipe also reminds us of some of the joys of eating and drinking. The smoker is sipping and absorbing an enchanted food, an Olympian ambrosia that gives itself to the nose and tongue instead of the stomach. Like a splendid morning mist, it marks the spectator with its beauty then vanishes as if it never were. This is the dry drink and chimerical food, whose magical consumption gave American Indians the power to go for days without actual food.

It is also a ritual. As surely as the taking of wafer and wine is a ritualistic reunion with the body of Christ, so is the consumption of this insubstantial smoky substance a reunion and merger with the source of warmth, comfort, and satisfaction. The tranquil pipe smoker is no longer a lonely individual standing apart from the world; he has abandoned his separate identity to merge with that transcendent and all-justifying giver of warmth, comfort, and pleasure. The man in the mackinaw is no longer *smoking* the pipe, he *is* the pipe.

In our world, nothing is perfect. Men and women can spend their entire lives without ever seeing, hearing, or experiencing anything that is complete, whole, and without blemish. Genuine fulfillment is, for many, something which they will never experience. But not for this gentleman, on this evening, before this fireplace. He is complete; he is whole and unblemished. And he is fulfilled, because he is experiencing a protracted moment of perfection. He is swimming in the Tao, balancing, adjusting, staying right in the center of his pleasure, locked in on the perfect puff.

The perfect puff is not something the smoker does; it is something he experiences in concert with his pipe. The pipe — every bit as alive and organic and unpredictable as the smoker — dictates exactly when and how much to puff. There is really no choice in the matter, perfection is imposed on the smoker. Once he has packed and lit the pipe, there is no backing out: the die is cast and the game must be played out, the dance must be completed, the ritual of loving-eating-drinking-merging must be carried out to its termination.

The perfect puff is a sensual and rhythmic *entente* between smoker and pipe, wherein the smoker takes from the pipe only enough of its offering to keep the pipe burning. The perfect puff is a sensitive counterpoint between the pipe and the pipe smoker; it accompanies the burning ember on its downward journey, each and every flake of tobacco gradually and totally consumed.

Still mesmerized and still deep within his reverie, the pipe smoker notes the deepening and enriching of the flavor as the tobacco burns down to the bottom of the bowl. The smoke is thicker, heavier, more powerful. The smoker keeps his rhythm steady and balanced because the end is near and the cycle is nearly complete.

The pace slows, the smoke thins a bit, gently dying away into nothingness. In the bowl is a layer of gray ash. There is nowhere left to go, nothing more to complete. The ritual is over and the dance is ended. All that is left is contentment.

14

THE CARE AND FEEDING
OF A PIPE

With Pipe after Pipe, we still keep in motion,
In Puffing and Smoking like Guns on the Ocean,
And when they are out, we charge 'em, and then
We stop 'em, and ram 'em and recharge agen. . . .

> — *Anonymous,* Mock Songs and
> Joking Poems, *1675*

A pipe has a personality of its own. Once it has been broken in and smoked for a few weeks, its character begins to emerge. It will have its own special aroma and its own taste, just as it will have a certain weight, shape, degree of coolness, and ease of draught.

But not only does a pipe have its own unique character; it also has a history. When a pipe smoker gazes at his pipe rack, he is surveying a group of friends, each of which has provided its own special companionship and satisfaction over the months and years. Deciding which pipe to smoke involves a subtle evaluation of the times spent with each pipe, bad times as well as good, bitter times as well as sweet. It is much like choosing a special companion for a special day.

A pipe is an organic thing with a life of its own. A pipe grows and changes, achieving great moments of bliss and plummeting moments of disappointment. As its history develops, anything can happen. It may last a lifetime or die a bitter death. Because of its organic delicacy, a pipe must be cared for and fed with considerable care and concern. The serious pipe smoker takes every precaution that his expensive Comoy does not become a foul-smelling, burnt-out furnace.

Resting the Pipe

No pipe smoker should have fewer than two pipes. Two is the minimum, because it is absolutely necessary to let a pipe rest and cool and aerate between smokes. Failure to do so will almost inevitably ruin the pipe. Most pipe smokers end up with more than two, for the simple reason that they are fascinated with the different personalities of pipes. New pipes are gradually added to the collection for the same reasons that new wives were once added to a harem.

The choices of materials for a pipe (briar, clay, meerschaum, cherrywood) and the shapes of a pipe (straight, bent, long, short, tall, squat) offer so many possibilities that a veteran pipe smoker may end up with dozens of pipes in his collection. But there are usually four or five that he uses constantly and that are his favorites. They get a lot of use, so they should accordingly receive a lot of care. Letting the pipe rest for at least an hour between smokes is a sound rule.

Cleaning the Pipe

When the smoker has finished his smoke, he should immediately empty and clean his pipe *while it is hot*. Not only must the ashes be tapped out, but all of the partially burned and unburned material — the dottle — must be removed from the bottom of the bowl. The reason for this is that when the pipe is still hot, the bowl of the pipe is porous and will absorb the remaining nicotine and tar. If the moist dottle is allowed to remain in the dead pipe, it will soak into the walls and stem. If this is repeated enough times, the pipe will gradually develop a tar and nicotine stench and a bitter taste. When this happens, the pipe, the pipe smoker, and the smoker's clothing will malodorously announce their fetid presence to all and sundry.

A smelly pipe smoker is a bad pipe smoker, fit to be ostracized from the fellowship of pipe smokers. Such a smoker is usually someone who habitually holds the entire bit in his mouth, clamping down on it like a cigar fancier with his stogie. This automatically causes increased salivation, and the liquid will steadily drop down the stem toward the bowl of the pipe where it will gurgle and belch like a witch's kettle. The bad pipe smoker lacks understanding of *dry puffing*, in which the stem barely touches the lips.

When saliva reaches the bowl end of the stem it mixes with the water, tar, and alkaloids that have been released from the tobacco. The most powerful of these alkaloids is nicotine, a colorless fluid that is not even 1 percent of the tobacco leaf; when heated in solution, however, it has an odor that is highly nauseating. If, at the end of the smoke, the pipe is left in an ashtray with its hot bowl and warm residue of tars and alkaloids remaining, the pipe will quickly become fouled.

Instead, the well-advised pipe smoker finishes his smoke by lightly tapping out the contents of the bowl against his palm or against the cork knob of his ashtray. He holds the pipe by the bowl when he taps it clear, not by the stem or the shank, for he does not want to risk breaking them. Very cautious pipe smokers always avoid hitting the bowl against anything and prefer, instead, to clean out the bowl with a pipe tool or wooden match.

Another sound rule is to clean both stem and shank while the pipe is hot. This is done with a pipe cleaner. A smoker must have on hand a large supply of pipe cleaners, and use them frequently and generously. These little devices of fiber and wire can help keep a pipe clean and sweet smelling.

One precaution is necessary: when cleaning a hot pipe, it is normally not advisable to try to pull or unscrew the stem from the shank. Because the stem and shank are made of different materials, they have different rates of expansion. If the stem and shank are tightly fitted, it is very possible that extra pressure on the heat-swollen materials will make something crack. Usually it is the shank which cracks, and the pipe is virtually ruined. If the stem is to be removed, bring pressure to bear only at the point where shank and stem are joined. Never hold the pipe by the bowl while twisting the bit with the other hand. With so much torque, the odds of breaking the pipe are very high.

The classic way of using a pipe cleaner is to leave the pipe intact, insert the cleaner into the bit, and push it slowly through the stem until it enters the shank and begins to curl up into the bottom of the bowl. If it can be done, one then takes the wire that is peeking into the bowl and continues to pull it on through. In this way the liquids are taken away from the bit and the entire shank and bowl bottom are cleaned. With this done, many pipe smokers then insert a new pipe cleaner all the way through the stem into the shank and leave it there while the pipe rests. The fibers of the cleaner will continue to absorb any remaining liquids.

If the stem can be easily removed without endangering the pipe, one can clean it separately from the shank. But it is essential to remember to put a pipe cleaner through the shank. A doubled-over pipe cleaner will clean the shank handily. If you are in a situation where pipe cleaners are unavailable, it is equally possible to use long grass, a chicken feather, or simply a tightly rolled piece of paper.

Even though cleaning after each use will guarantee a sweet smoke, your most frequently used pipes need a thorough cleaning and drying every few months or so. For this you will need some pipe sweetener, which is alcohol with some flavoring. These sweeteners are sold at any tobacconist. If you wish you can make your own by mixing pure grain alcohol with a tiny amount of an aromatic, such as

Figure 11. Billiard. The gently tapered walls of the Billiard and the gently fluted columns of the Parthenon are of the same classic simplicity. The classic briar pipe is the Billiard. Its simple elegance discloses a wall line that gradually thickens and swells toward the midline and then tapers back down at the bottom. This gives greatest insulation at the point where the greatest heat is generated in the Pipe, namely when the tobacco burn has reached the middle of the bowl. The heat diminishes again when the dottle is neared.

oil of wintergreen or oil of cloves. Other pipe smokers traditionally use brandy or rum for a thorough cleaning of their pipes. In a pinch, you can even use cologne. In a tighter pinch, you can use water (sparingly). The main thing is to dry out and air the pipe immediately after this internal bath.

The specific procedures can vary. The smoker may pour alcohol into the bowl, and then blow through the stem to make the liquid bubble for a while. Or the smoker may take a large mouthful of rum or brandy, put the stem to his lips with the bowl turned upside down, and blow the liquor explosively through the pipe. This not only scours the pipe but drenches and fouls the shirt of the smoker and any onlookers, so it is best to lean over a basin if one takes this drastic course. The least dramatic method is to pour the pipe sweetener into the bowl, letting it sit for a while with the stem tilted up.

Once the liquid has done its job, the smoker must thoroughly clean and dry the stem, shank, and bowl with pipe cleaners and a cloth, leaving the pieces to air for a day. The following day your pipe will be once again at its full potential.

Scraping Out the Bowl

After each smoke, a little more char will remain on the inside of the bowl. This char is invaluable to the flavor and heat distribution of the pipe, but too much char creates other problems, the greatest being that the cake can finally become so thick that there is hardly room in the bowl for the tobacco. Another problem that may occur is formation of an uneven cake (usually caused by a consistently unevenly filled pipe or by frequently smoking it where there are currents of wind which may expand or contract the bowl unevenly, causing cracking from the pressure). When the cake builds up too thickly or too unevenly, the pipe must be reamed out.

There are different opinions about which instrument is best used in scraping out unwanted cake. Some prefer a penknife, others prefer a metal reamer, still others file and chip away at the char. But there is no division of opinion on this point: whatever you do, don't scrape away all the cake and leave the bowl's inner wall naked. If one tiny spot of the cake has been cut through to the bare wall, all of the cake must be removed with extreme caution and one must start the tedious charring process all over again as if the pipe were brand new.

Perhaps the ideal instrument is a sharp metal pipe reamer, which is adjustable to any size bowl. By inserting the reamer in the bowl and carefully turning it, the carbon is gently scraped or razored off. The two main points to be observed in this operation are to ream the pipe walls and the bottom of the bowl with perfect evenness, lest the wall of the bowl crack or burn out; and to reduce the cake to 1/16th of an inch, about the thickness of a penny. Of course it is not necessary to wait until the char is an inch thick before reaming. It is just as well to keep the reamer handy and to maintain the cake at a steady 1/16th of an inch all the time.

Racking the Pipes

Because pipe smokers tend to collect pipes, they need a convenient way to store them. A rack full of one's favorite pipes is one of the visual delights of the pipe smoker, inviting him to appraise, inspect, and remember the different personalities of each member of his harem of assorted pipes.

Another value of a pipe rack is that it stores the pipes in a vertical position. But here again, the smoker has a choice: shall he store his pipe with the bowl up or the bowl down? With the stem upmost, any vagrant fluids in the pipe will drain downward into the bowl, making the next smoke a bit heavy and rough. But with the bowl upmost, the liquids will drain out of the bowl and into the stem. All smokers know that a drop of nicotine in the bit of a pipe can be overwhelmingly disagreeable if it touches the tongue. An obvious concern, then, is whether the pipe smoker should worry more about the sweetness of the bowl or the sweetness of the bit. The answer is that he worries about both, and so completely empties and cleans his pipe after each smoke, leaving a new pipe cleaner in it. If this is done each time, it does not matter which end of the pipe is up.

©Jonquille Albin

PART IV

THE GRAND
WORLD OF PIPES

15

FROM SOAPSTONE TO CALABASH GOURDS:
WHAT PIPES ARE MADE OF

*History books are full of great men who got more pleasure and satisfaction
out of a pipe than most anything. A pipe is the oldest form of enjoying tobacco,
and it's one of the most natural ways to smoke. A good pipe brings out the
flavor and aroma of the tobacco. There's something downright friendly about
a pipe. It seems to mellow a man . . . gives him ripeness of judgment and
warmth to his feelings.*

— A New Jersey pipe smoker

The most primitive smoking device is a hole in the ground. One
makes a depression in the dirt for the pipe "bowl," and then
inserts a stick through one wall, packing the dirt around it tightly,
and gently removing the stick to leave a draught hole for the "stem."
Of course one must stretch out on the ground to smoke an earth
pipe, and it certainly is not portable, two factors that probably
account for the lack of popularity.

Pipes can be made of virtually anything that can be shaped or
cupped. The list of materials used to make pipes is astonishing:
leaves, bamboo, gorse-root, a crab or lobster claw, clay, bone, horn,

limestone, soapstone, catlinite, slate, pottery, glass, porcelain, meerschaum, walrus tusks, shells, coconuts, gourds, iron, brass, copper, silver, gold, and hundreds of different woods.

This is a vast array of choices, but many of them are rather bad by contemporary standards. Of all the many substances available for making pipes, only a relative few produce a satisfying smoke, and these few have established themselves as favorites.

The Mayans of Central America smoked tobacco in a tube pipe — a long piece of wood, clay, or soft stone with a hole running its length, small at the stem end and large at the bowl end. This kind of pipe did not curve up at the bowl, so it was necessary to wedge something into the bowl to keep the tobacco from falling out.

The tube pipe is also used in India, Pakistan, Afghanistan, and other countries of the Middle East where it is called a *chillum*. Indian chillums are usually made of soapstone and are usually filled with ganja, a potent form of marijuana. The chillum is highly sanitary, inasmuch as it never touches the mouth. Instead, it is held in the hands, which are cupped together around its stem as the smoke is sucked between the fingers. Chillum smokers always look as if they are playing a harmonica.

The Mayans and other American Indians used the tube pipe in a special ceremony called "blowing over." One person lit the pipe, and instead of sucking in the smoke, blew the smoke out the other end, directly into the faces of an assembly of smokers, each of whom cupped his hands in harmonica-playing fashion to hold the smoke. The bas-relief carved on the right side of the Temple of the Cross in Palenque, Mexico, shows an old priest busily "blowing over" with his tube pipe, smoke pouring forth like great swirling serpents.

The North American Indians modified the tube pipe. With simple ingenuity, they made a curve at the end of it so that the bowl pointed upward rather than horizontally. Over a period of centuries, the form of the Indian pipe evolved until it became an object of high art and profound reverence. The celebrated calumet of the

North American Indians is a long, ornate instrument with a bowl of red stone and a decorated stem of ash wood. They used an ingenious and timesaving method to bore a hole through the long stem of the ash. The pith at one end of the branch was slightly hollowed out, a wood-boring grub worm was placed inside, and the hole was sealed up. The end of the stick where the grub worm sat was then held over a fire, thus inciting it to bore as fast as it could in the opposite direction. When it finally worked its way through the pith to the end of the branch, the worm had its freedom and the Indian had his air hole.

Many pipes are made of bamboo, and one of the most splendid specimens of bamboo pipes is the South Pacific *baubau*. Famous for the mellowness as well as potency of its smoke, the baubau is very different from ordinary pipes. A piece of bamboo a foot-and-a-half long and an inch-and-a-half in diameter, it has one hole for the bowl and one for the mouth. When the bowl is lit, the smoker sucks the smoke into the bamboo chamber until the interior is densely packed with smoke. Only then does he inhale the smoke and pass the pipe around for others to enjoy. During the 1960s the baubau became very popular in America as a communal marijuana pipe.

Another ingenious pipe is the *nargeeleh*, the original water pipe invented by the Persians. The word nargeeleh is Arabic for coconut, the shell of which supplies the body of the pipe. The nargeeleh consists of a coconut with a pipe bowl inserted in its top, a tube leading from the bowl down into the bottom of the coconut, which is half-filled with water or some fragrant liquid. In the side of the coconut, above the liquid, are one or more holes into which a thin cane can be inserted. When the bowl is lit the smoker sucks through the cane, creating a light vacuum in the airtight chamber; this draws the smoke down the tube into the water where it immediately bubbles back up and can be inhaled through the cane, water-cooled and fragrant.

The advantages of the nargeeleh are twofold: the cooling and cleansing of the smoke by the water creates a smoke of unexcelled mellowness; and the nargeeleh can be smoked by as many people as there are holes in the coconut to put a cane into. It is common in the Middle East to see a nargeeleh enthroned in the center of a cafe table, surrounded by enthusiastic gentlemen all of whom are puffing on long Malabar canes projecting from the sides of the pipe. When hashish was smoked, it was the custom to drink the hemp-stained water after the smoke was over. Often wealthy men would not smoke at all; instead, women would smoke the pipe until the water in it was strong enough for the men to drink.

The direct descendant of the nargeeleh is the renowned *hookah*, which may be made from glass, metal, or pottery, and is distinguished by the soft tubes which come out of the bowl. These tubes, called *narbeeshes*, are from two to thirty feet in length, thus allowing the smokers freedom to move away from the water pipe and recline in sumptuous bliss on a pile of pillows, all the while sucking on the serpentine tube.

The water pipe spread from Persia downward into Africa and eastward into China, where metalsmiths fashioned some of the most refined water pipes ever made, from materials such as brass, silver and gold, decorated with small sculptures and designs.

The tube pipe of the American Indians had its direct descendant in the English clay pipe, whose slightly tilted bowl resembles a tube pipe bent at the end. The English admired and used the white clay found around Dorsetshire. Highly porous, it literally soaked up the tars and liquids of the tobacco, making for an exceptionally dry smoke. Fanciers of clay pipes particularly enjoy the pure, earthy quality of the clay, for both the taste and aroma of a clay pipe are quite distinctively its own.

The only drawback to a clay pipe is that the bowl becomes extremely hot, so hot that it cannot be held. Thus all clay pipes have a small spur or knob on the bottom, for holding the pipe without burning the fingers.

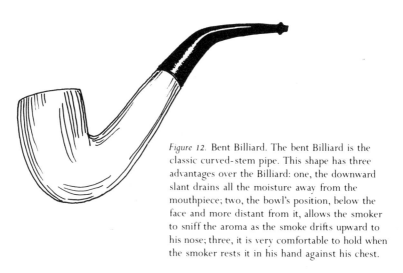

Figure 12. Bent Billiard. The bent Billiard is the classic curved-stem pipe. This shape has three advantages over the Billiard: one, the downward slant drains all the moisture away from the mouthpiece; two, the bowl's position, below the face and more distant from it, allows the smoker to sniff the aroma as the smoke drifts upward to his nose; three, it is very comfortable to hold when the smoker rests it in his hand against his chest.

Clay pipes became works of art in France. The French molded the clay bowl into magnificent *objets d'art*, decorating them with the likenesses of famous persons, animals, scenes, and symbols. The most famous of the French clay pipe designers was Gambier, whose name was once synonymous with pipes in France. The poets Malarmé, Rimbaud, and Baudelaire each smoked a Gambier.

Similar to clay pipes are those of porcelain, a ceramic made from the fine paste of kaolin, also called china clay. Its bowl is just as hot on the outside as it is on the inside, as it is with a clay pipe. Porcelain pipes are a specialty of the Alsatians, who came to make the bowl and shank of the pipe out of porcelain, with the stem of cherrywood and the bit of cow horn. This exotic combination of ingredients is found in the typical Alsatian pipe, which looks quite similar to a saxophone. The Alsatian is a spectacular pipe to have in a collection, but its porcelain bowl must be handled with great delicacy. If the pipe is cold, it must not be filled to the top and must not be smoked fast, for the extreme heat will cause the outer surface to develop little crack lines that eventually will ooze nicotine. But if care is taken at first, a browned and seasoned Alsatian will have a long life and can develop an opulent flavor. A special feature of the Alsatian is the traditional metal cap over the bowl, which controls burning if the smoker is in the wind.

The queen of pipes is the *meerschaum* (from the German for "sea foam"), a white, lightweight, and hydrous silicate of magnesia that is found principally in Turkey. Meerschaum is a highly porous mineral that has remarkable smoking properties once it has been processed by being boiled in milk and then kneaded with wax and linseed oil. A genuine meerschaum pipe is cut from a single block of the processed mineral. The softness of the material allows it to be easily carved, and many meerschaum pipes are stunning works of art that are handed down from father to son.

But the meerschaum is a most delicate pipe. Its queenly temperament demands more attention than many smokers care to give. As it is patiently smoked, the white hue slowly darkens to an amber, then a yellow ochre, eventually becoming a rich mahogany. This coloring of a meerschaum is one of its delights — and one of its bothers. While tempering it, for example, it is wise to smoke a meerschaum without touching its bowl with the bare fingers, lest it become unevenly colored. Another caveat is never to set a warm meerschaum on a cold surface for it just may crack. Do not smoke a meerschaum out of doors — this too will ruin the coloration. And it is important never to clean a meerschaum with alcohol or any commercial sweetener; the taste of the pipe will be irrevocably changed.

Meerchaums are also quite expensive, and when the stems are of amber and the bowl is carved the price may make you whistle. But meerschaums are not, in any case, for the beginning smoker. The beginner should start with a briar, and when the time is ripe, venture into a meerschaum. When he does so, he should bear in mind that the flavor he seeks is found only in a genuine block meerschaum. If the pipe is presented as "pressed meerschaum" or something similar, it will not be worth the price no matter how cheap the pressed meerschaum may be.

Because of its high porosity, meerschaum is sometimes used to line the inner walls of briar. And quite frequently a gleaming meerschaum bowl is set into the gaping maw of a calabash gourd to make the pipe that was Sherlock Holmes's favorite. Indeed, the calabash is the favorite of many pipe smokers. Its huge chamber cools the air once it is drawn through the bowl into the gourd, producing a mellifluous, utterly comforting puff.

Throughout the eighteenth and early nineteenth centuries, a meerschaum was *the* pipe to smoke. The aristocrats and the *nouveaux riches* smoked this queen of pipes, and the commoners and poor smoked the jack of pipes, clay. The two finally were supplanted during the second decade of the nineteenth century by the arrival of the king of pipes: the briar.

As is so frequently the case with such things, the briar pipe was discovered by accident. Sometime after the death of Napoleon, a French pipe maker made a pilgrimage that was taken by many an admirer of the deceased Emperor: he visited the Mediterranean island of Corsica where Napoleon was born. During the visit he broke his meerschaum pipe, the only pipe he had brought. Distressed, he asked a woodcarver to make him a pipe of wood. The local wood used by the carver was that of the heath tree, a hardy, shrubby evergreen that grows well in the Mediterranean's rocky, sandy, arid soil. The carver presented this light but tremendously hard little pipe to the visitor, who was properly amazed at its qualities. The visitor had seen other pipes, made of sweet-smelling cherrywood, rosewood, and other materials, but although wood is a poor heat conductor (unlike clay and meerschaum), it is not very fire resistant. Eventually, wood pipes will burn out, just like a fragrant Missouri corncob pipe. But the walls of the little Corsican briar pipe took on a light char, sealing the wood and creating a most agreeable smoke.

Delighted, the pipe maker asked for some pieces of the wood, which in French is called *bruyére* (hence our use of the word "briar"). Upon arriving back at home, he sent the briar blocks to the factory in Saint-Claude in eastern France, which turned wooden pipe stems for his own pipe business. This time he asked the Saint-Claude carvers, famous for their work with small wooden objects, to turn as many pipes as they could make from the briar block.

This was the beginning of a saga that established Saint-Claude as the Mecca of briar pipe production for all true believers. The methods and machinery developed there have gradually spread all over the world, as have the skilled pipe makers of Saint-Claude — some of the finest "London Made" pipes are indeed made in London, and are certainly made by French craftsmen.

The tremendous knotty hardness of the briar is due not only to the root's struggle with rock and aridity, but also to long time spent in this struggle: from sixty to two hundred years. Its position as king of pipes rests upon its fire resistance, its low heat conductivity, its high porosity, and its combination of strength and lightness. If the meerschaum were not so easily broken we might never have discovered just how tough the briar is.

16

THE GEOMETRY OF PIPES:
HOW PIPES ARE MADE

A Ballade of the Best Pipe

In vain you fervently extole,
    In vain you puff, your cutty clay.
A twelvemonth smoked and black as coal,
'Tis redolent of rank decay,
The bones of monks long passed away —
    A fragrance I do not admire;
And so I hold my nose and say,
Give me a finely seasoned briar.

Macleod, whose judgment on the whole
    Is faultless, has been led astray
To nurse a high-born meerschaum bowl,
For which he sweetly had to pay.
Ah, let him nurse it as he may,
    Before the colour mounts much higher,
The grate shall be its fate one day.
    Give me a finely seasoned briar,

The heathen Turk of Istamboul,
    In oriental turban gay,
Delights his unbelieving soul
With hookahs, bubbling in a way
To fill a Christian with dismay
    And wake the old Crusading fire.
May no such pipe be mine, I pray
    Give me a finely seasoned briar.

Clay, meerschaum, hookah, what are they
    That I should view them with desire?
Both now, and when my hair is grey,
    Give me a finely seasoned briar.

— R. F. Murray,
The Scarlet Gown, *1891.*

*A*ll things considered, the ideal pipe is a briar: it is tougher than a meerschaum, cooler to hold than a clay, and more fire-resistant than a cherrywood or corncob pipe. Until the discovery of briar, the ideal pipe was a meerschaum, and it was owned only by the wealthy. But when briar pipes came on the scene, everyone — wealthy or not — could afford to have the ideal pipe.

At first briar pipes were carved by hand, like meerschaums; but eventually the canny wood-turners of Saint-Claude developed specialized machinery for the complex task of turning out well-carved pipes. The French produced hundreds of thousands of medium-priced pipes on their high-speed lathes and frazing machines. Price was no longer a barrier and soon the briar pipe became the standard of the pipe smoking fraternity.

At first, briar was taken from southern France (especially the eastern Pyrenees) and Corsica. Eventually briar was found in Algeria, Spain, Sicily, Sardinia, Greece, and elsewhere along the Mediterranean coast. The heath tree itself is useless for pipe making; only the burl can serve this purpose. The burl is a bulbous stump, lying just beneath the ground, which anchors the trunk of the tree against the wrenching winds of the Mediterranean and serves as the gathering point of the root system.

Only the side sections of the burl make good pipe material; the central section is part of the tree trunk and root system, and is ordinary wood. In the side sections, however, the grain of the wood becomes densely packed, whorled, and gnarled, and this is where the great pipes lie, awaiting only the turner's art to bring them into being.

The minimum age of a heath tree for pipe making is about thirty or forty years. At that delicate age, the burl is still small and will yield only a few pipes. But the older heath trees develop burls of impressive size, from ten to thirty inches in width and depth, the largest weighing as much as five hundred pounds.

Suppliers of burls believe that long-dead heath trees contain the best burls. A few years of dormancy in the harsh soil dries out the burl to rock hardness, free of sap that might turn up in a finished pipe to spoil its flavor. So if the digger brings up a burl from a living tree, it must first be dried. Fresh burls are laid in long trenches and covered with damp earth and straw, so that they will dry slowly.

Once dry, the burls are sliced up into small blocks called *ebauchons*. The ebauchons are about three inches long, the size of the pipe bowl and stem they are destined to become. A good-sized burl will yield about fifty ebauchons. After they are sliced by a circular saw, the blocks are put through a curing process to remove all possible tars and resins. The curing is commonly done by boiling the blocks from one to two days, perhaps in a mixture of peanut oil and beeswax. Some manufacturers prefer that the ebauchons be baked under controlled heat to sweat out the tars and resins. Their line of reasoning is that the resultant wood will be more porous and thus heat resistant.

Once they are cured, the blocks are put in special drying rooms where they are kept from several months to several years. When they are bone-dry, they are graded and placed into burlap bags for shipment to the pipe manufacturer. Each bag contains from sixty to eighty-five dozen blocks and weighs about 170 pounds.

Upon arrival at the factory, the briar blocks are inspected carefully for flaws, which are common in a wood as uneven in texture and density as that of the heath tree burl. But the briar burl may also be defective because it has stones inside. As the wood slowly and tortuously grows in the ungenerous and arid soil, it frequently meets a pebble and gradually engulfs it, incorporating it into the burl. At any stage in the carving of the briar, the cutting machines may encounter such a small stone, embedded so that it makes the wood valueless as a pipe. Pipe makers are resigned to the problem of defective briar blocks, and they feel they are lucky if they are able to get three top-grade pipes out of a thousand ebauchons.

When the usable ebauchons have been selected, they are put into a special woodworking lathe to shape the bowl. This is a most exacting operation whereby the revolving bit carves out both the inside and outside of the bowl. The shape and thickness of the walls will vary according to the design used. Shaping the bowl is also a mechanically difficult task for the machine. Despite their hardness, the cutting blades are rapidly dulled by the tough briar and require frequent resharpening.

The next step in making the pipe is to shape the shank and round out the bottom of the bowl. The shank may be thick, thin, round, square, oval, straight, or curved, depending on the traditional style desired. The frazing machines that cut out these specific shapes operate very much like a machine for duplicating keys; that is, a model is clamped onto the machine, which follows its shape exactly as it cuts the line of the shank.

At this stage the ebauchon looks like a pipe and shank, except that there is no air hole. Boring the shank so that the hole is in its exact center and in the exact direction of the bowl's bottom is a task for only the most highly skilled pipe makers. A power drill is used to bore the hole, which is normally a little over one inch long and cut to within a tolerance of no less than 1/500 of an inch. After the air hole is finished, the mortise is reamed out of the shank's end, where the stem of the pipe will fit.

From this point on, the pipe and stem are shaped with increasingly finer grades of sandpaper. Most pipes are then stained to bring out the clarity of the grain, and further refined by buffing with a cloth wheel. The buffed pipe is then polished with a special compound called tripoli, and finely rubbed with fine carnauba wax to preserve the finish.

By these meticulous procedures, the classically lustrous finish of the briar pipe is created. On occasion some steps are skipped over, so that the bowl of the pipe will be rough, a style variously called thorn, rustic, relief, or shell. The rough effect is achieved by sandblasting the briar, which cuts away the softer portions of the wood, leaving only the hardest surfaces. This gives the pipe the texture of a walnut shell, making it better able to dissipate heat and thus cooler to hold.

The stem is fashioned next. Just as the ideal material for a pipe bowl is briar, the ideal material for the stem is the hard rubber called vulcanite or ebonite. Vulcanite is essentially tasteless and long-wearing, and it is also very versatile in the many shapes it can take. Due to its sensitivity to heat, a warmed vulcanite stem can be bent into any desired shape. If a smoker wishes to create a curve in his vulcanite stem, he can do so by holding the stem over steam for a few minutes before gently shaping it. It should be completely cool before being inserted into the shank; if it is still hot the shank may crack.

Vulcanite stems are made either by compression molding or injection molding. In the first instance, vulcanite powder is heated and compressed into stem halves. The halves are bonded together with heat and then the bonded edge is sanded and polished until it is invisible. In the second procedure, molten rubber is injected into a die under high pressure, then quickly cooled in water. When the die is opened, a perfectly shaped stem is revealed.

Once the shank is bored and the tenon of the stem is fitted into the mortise, the pipe looks odd: although the bowl is symmetrically shaped, the stem, at this stage, is much bigger than the shank, and must be sanded down to the proper size. All of the final sanding and polishing operations are done with the stem firmly fitted into the shank. In this fashion the final juncture of shank and stem is absolutely smooth. Pipe smokers will notice that stem and shank are often so exactly aligned in one position, that a 90-degree turn of the stem will put the stem out of alignment with the shank. It fits only in one position. If you bought two fine pipes of exactly the same style and attempted to switch the stems, you would likely discover that they do not interchange. The stem is made for one pipe and one pipe only.

From the digging of the briar burl to the final coat of carnauba wax, the making of a fine briar pipe requires great attention, high skill, and considerable experience. Like Rome, a pipe is not built in a day; the many steps between conception and completion are the careful stages of a laborious process. Given the prodigious amount of labor and intelligence required, it is not surprising that a fine briar is expensive. But as the pipe smoker stands in the pipe shop gazing down at the lustrous little work of art lying snugly in its pipe case, beckoning to him with its aromatic promise, he understands that it is not expensive at all.

PART V

THE RELIGIOUS
AND SYMBOLIC
ASPECTS OF
PIPE SMOKING

17

THE SENSUOUS SYMBOLISM
OF PIPE SMOKING

See, I fill this sacred pipe with the bark of the red Willow; but before we smoke it, you must see how it is made and what it means. These four ribbons hanging here on the stem are the four quarters of the universe. The black one is for the west where the thunder beings live to send us rain; the white one for the north, whence comes the great white cleansing wind; the red one for the east, whence springs the light and where the morning star lives to give men wisdom; the yellow for the south, whence come the summer and the power to grow.

But these four spirits are only one Spirit after all, and this eagle feather here is for that One, which is like a father, and also it is for the thoughts of men that should rise high as eagles do. Is not the sky a father and the earth a mother, and are not all living things with feet or wings or roots their children? And this hide upon the mouthpiece here, which should be bison hide, is for the earth, from whence we came and at whose breast we suck as babies all our lives, along with all the animals and birds and trees and grasses. And because it means all this, and more than any man can understand, the pipe is holy.

—Black Elk, Sioux medicine man

*A*lthough little more than a portable furnace with a reed stuck into it, a pipe has a powerful effect on a human being. The transformatory effects of pipe smoking are well known and well chronicled.

The pipe offers a complete sensuous experience. It affects all five human senses: seeing, touching, tasting, smelling, and hearing. Pipe smoking is a veritable cornucopia of sensations.

The visual aspects of the pipe are considerable. The shape of the pipe excites the eye, and the shapes and styles of pipes are wide ranging and provocative. Shape is abetted by color, generally earthen tones. Wood is dark and brown, earth is dark and brown, and so is the pipe. Even nonwood pipes such as clay and meerschaum gradually brown over the months. This earthen color identifies the pipe as something both primal and organic. And when we add another visual factor—the luster—this dark, primeval object asserts its full personality. The bowl may be shiny and smooth, glowing like a smoky jewel, or it may be rough-finished and mysterious. But the shape, color, and luster of the pipe establish only a minimal identity. Its fuller reality unfolds only as we build our appreciation through our other senses.

It is through touching and holding the pipe that its full three-dimensionality is realized. Seen, it has one grade of reality; touched, it communicates its full presence. The smooth round lines of a pot or apple briar are already intriguing to the eye; but when that shape is resting in the palm, its fuller meaning is disclosed. It is pleasant to fold one's hand around a smooth, rounded surface. The hand has an ancient familiarity with this form: from birth onward, human hands touch rounded flesh and take delight in this contact. That the pipe may be made of wood is no deterrent, for the mind carries associations of the pipe's shape with the beloved contours of a mother's face, the roundness of a shoulder or a breast.

This association of the feel of a pipe shape to the feel of a part of the body becomes inevitable when we add two other tactile factors, texture and warmth. The most popular texture of a pipe bowl is smooth, just like human skin. When that smoothness becomes warm, when lit, it becomes a sensual reminder of the warmth of the human body. When pipe smokers repeatedly refer to their pipe as a companion and friend, we must understand that they have been slowly beguiled into perceiving the pipe as a living being. With another tactile factor, the weight of the pipe, the tactile experience achieves extraordinary richness.

If the living, three-dimensional reality of a pipe is founded on visual and tactile factors, the indwelling spirit of the pipe begins to disclose itself as its vapors reach the nose. The fragrant, compelling

Figure 13. Canadian. This shape features an unusually long briar shank with a very short vulcanite bit. The functional advantage is that wood absorbs heat more quickly than vulcanite, and thus the more wood in the shank and stem the cooler the smoke. But this great length of briar around the air hole has another advantage: it seasons the smoke with a dry and subtle nut flavor that is unique among briar pipes.

cloud of tobacco smoke has an almost universal attraction; it is rich, sweet, comforting, and natural. When a pipe smoker walks by, he even dazzles the noses of others. The divine herb of the Indians has magic properties that console and entrance the entire olfactory system, triggering a desire (fortunately not a requirement) to inhale the smoke, drawing it fully into the lungs, letting it become a part of oneself.

It is with the aroma that the marriage of pipe and pipe smoker begins, but it is with the taste that the marriage is consummated. The taste of pipe tobacco smoke is unique. It simply *is* what it *is*. The fumes from the tobacco leaf are indescribably pleasant and comforting, like mother's milk. Yet the taste is a taste only; there is little substance, little is absorbed. It is neither eating nor drinking, but the smoker consumes this wondrous taste as if it were ambrosial food and drink. In tasting the smoke, the essence of the pipe's body is sucked into the body of the smoker and incorporated within him.

The smoker is symbolically taking in nourishment from a beloved companion.

The union of pipe smoker with pipe through the consumption of its smoke is rendered more subtle by the presence of another sense: hearing. It is significant that pipe smokers do not like noisy pipes; a gurgling, muck-filled pipe stem is as much an offense to the ears as it is a threat to the tongue. Instead, pipe smokers prefer a sound that approaches silence. The quiet, steady rhythm of the puff is a light sucking sound. The gentle bubbling of a water pipe is as much sound as most smokers can tolerate, and many smokers avoid water pipes as too noisy.

The beloved sound for the pipesmoker is the barely perceptible rhythm of the puff. Once the smoker has settled into that intoxicating rhythm he goes into a profound trance. Nothing moves except the mouth. The smoker seeking the perfect puff will lock in on this pulse, milking it slowly and assiduously until the flame has descended to the moist dottle at the bottom of the bowl.

How organic this rhythm is can be realized when we remember that there is also a sixth sense involved. The sixth sense is the proprioceptive sense, which gives us the sensations of our internal bodily world. The proprioceptive sense lets us know the position of the joints and the state of our muscular contraction. This inner bodily sensation of the pipe smoker is as silent as it is powerful. As he puffs, the smoker is internally aware that his body is in a most special posture: the arm is out, the elbow bent, the hand is near the face with the palm upward. This position helps round out the sensuous cornucopia of pipe smoking. The position of the pipe smoker's arm is similar to that of an infant going to sleep. At the most elemental level, the pipe smoker is reminded of the way in which he first experienced life and the sustenance of life: by sucking the nourishing breast of the mother, man's first companion. The breast of the mother is life-giving, and it is simultaneously pleasure-giving — a fact that permeates the child's life up until the nascent fires of puberty direct the youth to seek those same pleasures outside the family circle.

Sexuality, nourishment, and protective love are all primary needs of the human being, and during the history of a man's life these three hungers become united. This is evident from the fact that an adult male will normally have little interest in sucking until he becomes sexually aroused. When this occurs, the sexual needs trigger the unconscious memory, and the sucking reflex is activated.

If love, food, and sex are fundamental human needs, then these needs should not be forgotten. The pipe smoker daily reminds himself of these biological verities by a ritual of remembrance by smoking his pipe. During the ritual of its sacrificial burning, the pipe and its precious essence are transmuted into something halfway between inert substance and living flesh. During the fifteen or twenty minutes of pulsating bliss, the little heated object is magically transformed into an ancient, always supportive companion who generously gives warmth and nourishment.

Pipe smoking is a celebration and a reminder of the deeper roots which bind us to the human race and to the earth. The great Oglala Sioux visionary, Black Elk, knew this complex symbolism better than perhaps anyone else. The meanings of the pipe reach beyond the earth and reach even beyond the present and the past: "And because it means all this, and more than any man can understand, the pipe is holy."

18

SACRED AND PROFANE
PIPE SMOKING

And as she sang there came from her mouth a white cloud that was good to smell. Then she gave something to the chief, and it was a pipe with a bison calf carved on one side to mean the earth that bears and feeds us, and with twelve eagle feathers hanging from the stem to mean the sky and the twelve moons, and these were tied with a grass that never breaks. "Behold!" she said. "With this you shall multiply and be a good nation. Nothing but good shall come from it. Only the hands of the good shall take care of it and the bad shall not even see it."

—Black Elk, "The Offering of the Pipe"

For American Indians, particularly those of the plains, the pipe is a religious object accorded the highest reverence. Among the Sioux it is the ornately symbolical calumet that serves as the sacred instrument in major ceremonies—prayers, invocations, solemn agreements, and healings.

There are few spectacles so riveting as that of a medicine man standing amidst his people, pointing the calumet in the four compass directions in order to summon the four great spirits of the world to the community's aid. He holds the pipe upward toward the heavens and calls out to the sky, "Behold, O *Wakan-Tanka*! We are now about to do thy will. With all the sacred beings of the universe, we offer to You this pipe!"

He then takes a pinch of sacred tobacco (*kinnikinnik*, a mixture of tobacco, sumac leaves, and the inner bark of willow or dogwood), points it and the pipe stem directly west and calls out, "With this *wakan* tobacco, we place You in the pipe, O winged Power of the west. We are about to send our voices to *Wakan-Tanka*, and we wish You to help us!" The pinch of tobacco is now impregnated with the Power of the western spirit. The medicine man places the Power of the west into the pipe.

He takes another pinch of kinnikinnik and holds it and the pipe toward the north, whence come the cold and purifying airs. He prays the Bald-headed Eagle of the north to become part of the pipe offering to the ultimate deity, then places its power into the pipe. He makes the same invocation to *Huntka*, the long-winged Being of the east from whom comes light and wisdom. Then he addresses the White Swan of the south and requests that her ardent presence be part of the pipe.

The four quarters of the universe having been addressed, he solemnly takes a final pinch of kinnikinnik and points it and the stem directly downward at the earth, sacred earth from which we have all come and from which we are all nourished. "Grandmother and Mother Earth who bear fruit, for you there is a place in this pipe. . . . Help us! All together as one we cry: help us!"[14]

The powers of the physical universe are now compressed within the dull red bowl of the calumet — the dull red of blood, ancient and long remembered. The four corners of the earth and the earthly fundament itself have now been invoked as a unit. Only one dimension is missing: it is the upward direction of the heavens that cover and encompass the four corners of the world and its earthly fundament. There in the depths of the sky, remote, unreachable, and sovereign dwells the Universal Power, the One who has the power to answer the community's prayer. There is only one way to reach that remote One: through the smoke of the sacred pipe, which will enter the prayerful body of the tribe's spokesman and then be poured out again into the air where it rises upward, thinning and thinning and thinning into invisibility, rising upward toward the One, thinning itself into a refinement suitable for the invisible Universal Power in its rarefied abode.

Thus does a North American Indian symbolically draw the full and complete powers of the physical universe into the tiny bowl of the sacred calumet. There is no need for church, altar, chalice, cross, and the many accoutrements of the Christian tradition; all that is needed is the calumet. It is more than sufficient for the purpose of bringing a human request unto the throne of the One God.

The burnt offering, whose smoky essence rises to the gods, is the most ancient of all religious rituals. From the burnt viscera of the Greek sacrificial lamb to the votive candles twinkling before a Christian statue, it has always been mysterious flame and smoke that have connected mortal humans with the immortal gods. In many senses, the sacred pipe of the Indians is the most ingenious religious artifact ever invented.

It is not the smoke itself that, alone, suffices. It depends on what the smoke is made of. In every case it must be the fumy essence of something so precious that the gods will accept the offering. For the American Indians, no substance was so precious or so divine as that of sacred tobacco.

Because of its divine origins, tobacco was not only of value as an offering to the One but also as a gift to humankind. Mixed with other ingredients, a poultice of tobacco placed on top of a wound or abrasion would surely cure that affliction. Also the very smoking of tobacco was in itself health-giving, and this Indian belief in the salubrious qualities of tobacco smoke was fully accepted by Europeans who saw it as a panacea capable of curing anything from Catherine de Medici's headaches to James I's intestinal disorders.

It is generally the case that among primitive peoples religion and medicine are inseparable: What is potent for one purpose is potent for another. The curative potency of tobacco was thus employed in two ways: as a physical medicine and as a ritual to effect curing.

So it was the power of tobacco that impressed the Indians. It had the power to invoke all the spirits, to cure all ills, to fulfill all wishes and to assuage all hearts. They believed that if one mixed tobacco with ground shells and packed the mix into pills, one could live up to a week on these alone without any other food.

But the power of the sacred herb was nowhere more evident than the power *felt* by those who drew the smoke into their bodies. From a modern and profane point of view, pipe smoking brings pleasure. But from a primitive and sacred point of view, what one feels is religious transcendence. Through inhalation of the essential smoke, a transforming power suffuses throughout the body and spirit bringing awareness of a different reality.

Since the 1960s, altered states of consciousness and mind-altering substances have been lively topics for scientific and popular attention. Alcohol is a mind-altering substance, as are coffee, marijuana, cocaine, betel nuts, LSD, and scores of other substances, natural or artificial. Tobacco has always been recognized as this kind of substance, and this is a major part of its attraction. During the 1960s and 1970s, mind-altering drugs were normally used with a profane spirit of seeking pleasure, with nothing religious about the custom. But as the popularity of these substances spread beyond the youth culture, a curious event took place: rather than thinking of the mind-altering experience as a profane pleasure, more and more persons believed it to be a sacred transcendence wherein new realities were revealed. Rather than serving as an escape *from* reality, these drugs were thought of as an entryway *to* reality in its higher manifestations.

This new religiously oriented view of altered states of consciousness was buttressed by such works as Carlos Castaneda's saga of the Yaqui sorcerer, Don Juan, an Indian who knows that religious visions and altered states are the same thing. But a different confirma-

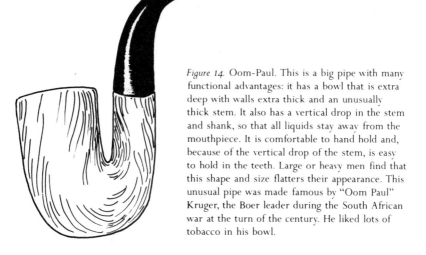

Figure 14. Oom-Paul. This is a big pipe with many functional advantages: it has a bowl that is extra deep with walls extra thick and an unusually thick stem. It also has a vertical drop in the stem and shank, so that all liquids stay away from the mouthpiece. It is comfortable to hand hold and, because of the vertical drop of the stem, is easy to hold in the teeth. Large or heavy men find that this shape and size flatters their appearance. This unusual pipe was made famous by "Oom Paul" Kruger, the Boer leader during the South African war at the turn of the century. He liked lots of tobacco in his bowl.

tion of the values of altered states of consciousness also came from modern psychology. During the 1970s, psychologists and other professionals such as Andrew Weil and Charles Tart deepened Abraham Maslow's belief that the revelations of "peak experiences" were essential to human health and growth.

Human beings need peak experiences and transcendent states in order to have calm spirits, clear minds and relaxed bodies. America has been virtually invaded by Asian gurus, all of whom have the same general message: meditate, and thereby become liberated from the tensions and constraints of ordinary consciousness. It is curious that the Eastern masters came to the Western Hemisphere to repeat what the American Indians had said and done long before their voices were smothered by the conquering European Americans. It is to Carlos Castaneda's credit that he reinserted into American consciousness the profound religious vision of the native North Americans.

But what was learned during the 1970s by an entire generation was the same thing that had been individually learned by solitary pipe smokers during the course of several centuries. Even though Europeans and white Americans learned to smoke the pipe without any religious instruction, all of them discovered—as all dedicated pipe smokers discover—that a well-smoked pipe is a transcendent experience that leaves the mind rested and the body relaxed. To smoke a pipe is to seek a gentle intoxication that relieves us of the burden of ordinary reality. The religious qualities of pipe smoking, first discovered by the North American Indians, are the same qualities discovered by all pipe smokers whether they realize it or not. Pipe smoking is always something more than the profane search for pleasure. The bliss into which the smoker is absorbed is clear evidene of his altered state, and he drifts into a transcendent state without ever realizing that it may be considered "religious."

To understand any great tradition, we must go back to its origins. To appreciate the tradition of pipe smoking we must always go back to the American Indians who originated it. No better reminder of the original spirit of pipe smoking can be found than in "The Offering of the Pipe," as spoken by Black Elk, the Oglala Sioux medicine man:

> Now I light the pipe, and after I have offered it to the powers that are one Power, and sent forth a voice to them, we shall smoke together. Offering the mouthpiece first of all to the One above—so—I send a voice:
>
> Hey hey! hey hey! hey hey! hey hey! . . .
>
> This is my prayer; hear me! The voice I have sent is weak, yet with earnestness I have sent it. Hear me!
>
> It is finished. *Hetchetu Aloh!*
>
> Now, my friend, let us smoke together so that there may be only good between us.[16]

REFERENCES

I enjoy blowing smoke, and I have been smoking a pipe for twenty-five years. Now I have about twenty-five of them. I feel this is the only way one should smoke: just blowing the smoke and getting the smell of the tobacco.

— A North Carolina pipe smoker

1. Brown, Joseph Epes. *The Sacred Pipe: Black Elk's Account of the Seven Rites of the Oglala Sioux.* Norman: U. Oklahoma Press, 1953, p. 21.
2. Shean, Burton. "The Pipe Wears Many Hats" in *Wonderful World of Pipes*, Vol. I, No. 2 (n.d.), pp. 68-70.
3. deKadt Marketing and Research, Inc. "Pipe Smoker Survey: Time Research Report #1661" (n.d., n.p.).
4. Criswell, Eleanor. "The Criswell Survey No. 1: A Study on the Social Image of Pipe Smoking." New York: Venturi, Inc., 1973.
5. Dunn, Tom, Ed. *The Pipe Smoker's Ephemeris*, published by The Universal Coterie of Pipe Smokers, 20-37 120th Street, College Point, N.Y. 11356. An interesting newsletter is published quarterly by The Sir Walter Raleigh Pipe Smoker's Club, Box SWR, Half Moon Bay, CA 94019.

REFERENCES

6. Campbell, Joseph. *The Portable Jung*. New York: Viking Press, 1971, p. 183.
7. *ibid.*, p. 180.
8. *ibid.*, p. 179.
10. Eysenck, H. J. *Readings on Basic Psychological Processes*. New York: Wiley-Interscience, 1971, p. 3.
11. *ibid.*, p. 136.
12. Benson, Herbert. *The Relaxation Response*. New York: Avon Books, 1976, pp. 159-61.
13. Brown, Barbara. *Stress and the Art of Biofeedback*. New York: Harper and Row Publishers, 1977, p. 229.
14. Sherman, Milton M. *All About Tobacco*. Woodside, N.Y.: P. M. Sherman Corp., 1970, pp. 32-3.
15. Herment, Georges. *The Pipe*. New York: Simon and Schuster, 1972, p. 49.
16. Neihardt, John G. *Black Elk Speaks: Being the Life Story of a Holy Man of Oglala Sioux*. New York: Pocket Books, 1972, pp. 4-5.